Play for Children with Special Needs

There are many more children with learning differences and difficulties in our schools today. Their needs are varied and complex, and professionals must find appropriate ways to enhance their learning. The value of play is endorsed internationally in policy initiatives including the Early Years Foundation Stage curriculum and Scotland's Curriculum for Excellence, so professionals can be reassured that 'more time to play' is in line with the latest thinking.

Christine Macintyre emphasises the importance of creating an environment where children become confident, independent learners, increasingly able to use their imaginations, care for others and to take safe risks. This fully revised edition of *Play for Children with Special Needs* includes new research findings and explains their implications for practice.

This book then enables those supporting children to:

- understand the benefits of play and adapt different scenarios to support children who do not find it easy to play;
- observe children as they play so that any difficulties can be identified early;
- analyse different play areas so that the different kinds of learning (intellectual, creative, motor, social and emotional) are appreciated.

Play for Children with Special Needs, second edition enables practitioners to appreciate the contribution that play makes to the education of all children, whether they have special needs or not. It is for parents, teachers, teaching assistants and nursery professionals as well as those who care for children at home.

Christine Macintyre is an educational consultant and prolific author, formerly at the Moray House School of Education, Edinburgh University.

Play for Children with Special Needs

Supporting children with learning differences, 3–9

Second edition

Christine Macintyre

Routledge
Taylor & Francis Group

LONDON AND NEW YORK

First edition published in Great Britain in 2002 by David Fulton Publishers

This edition published 2010
by Routledge
2 Park Square, Milton Park, Abingdon, Oxon OX14 4RN

Simultaneously published in the USA and Canada
by Routledge
270 Madison Avenue, New York, NY 10016

Routledge is an imprint of the Taylor & Francis Group, an informa business

© 2002, 2010 Christine Macintyre

Typeset in Sabon by
Keystroke, Tettenhall, Wolverhampton
Printed and bound in Great Britain by
TJ International Ltd, Padstow, Cornwall

British Library Cataloguing in Publication Data
A catalogue record for this book is available from the British Library

Library of Congress Cataloging-in-Publication Data
Macintyre, Christine, 1938–
   Play for children with special needs : supporting children with learning differences, 3–9/Christine Macintyre. — 2nd ed.
       p. cm.
   1. Learning disabled children—Education. 2. Play. I. Title.
   LC4704.M27 2009
   371.9′0472—dc22   2009025278

ISBN 10: 0–415–55884–0 (hbk)
ISBN 10: 0–415–55883–2 (pbk)
ISBN 10: 0–203–86364–X (ebk)

ISBN 13: 978–0–415–55884–6 (hbk)
ISBN 13: 978–0–415–55883–9 (pbk)
ISBN 13: 978–0–203–86364–0 (ebk)

Contents

Figures

Tables

Foreword

Having read and digested Christine Macintyre's excellent book *Play for Children with Special Needs*, my memory was drawn to the lectures of Professor Stanley Unwin which were broadcast on BBC radio over twenty years ago. He shared some similarities with Christine: his ideas were always passionately delivered and utterly convincing. Very few listeners would switch off once the professor began to speak, enjoying his enthusiasm to explain the complicated. He had a self-confidence and belief in what he was saying and was eager to share and define his philosophy with those who did not know or understand. However, there the similarities end.

After 5 or 10 minutes of Unwin's broadcast, it began to dawn upon the listener that the professor was talking complete rubbish. He used phrases that were muddled, sentences that were confusing and words that did not exist. All his ideas were incredibly obtuse and essentially everything he said was utterly meaningless. He was a comedian. The audience enjoyed being duped. Christine Macintyre is certainly none of the above!

It has been a pleasure to come across the second edition of Christine's book. No over-complicated new Ofsted pilot scheme documents here. No 'pie in the sky and cake tomorrow' touch by this fine educationalist. Rather than mincing flowery words with pretentious proposals, she focuses upon play, learning difficulties and the central issues of early years education. From the outset it is clear that this book is one for the reader, grounded in actual learning environments and situations, and not merely an outpouring of research championing the academic prowess of the author.

It is, of course, founded upon sound academic findings, but at every turn the child, the home and/or the school setting is the central focus. There is a snap in Macintyre's writing that cuts through the jargon and platitudes associated with many education books. Her succinct style gives pace to the book; she makes her point and moves on:

> Listen to Brooklyn who is a nursery nurse . . .
> Watch the children . . .
> Try to avoid minor upsets so that the child's name is not always being called out.
> For children who cannot focus, try this . . .
> What do we actually do to support dyspraxic children?
> How do we differentiate between work and play?

Macintyre's poem 'Please Give Me Time' is a stunning beginning to this book. I can think of none better, a manifesto for time, space, adaptability and understanding in a child's life. Many fine educational books tend to miss such issues, preferring the motor manual, the prescriptive approach. So thank you, Christine, for the warmth, insight and information with which this publication is richly endowed. And finally a thank-you to the children, parents, carers and teachers whose experiences Christine observed and shared, contributing to a book which will bring insight and education to many readers. This book encompasses a rare wealth of experience and knowledge and should be read by everyone involved in early years education.

Peter Dixon
Poet, Author, Artist, Teacher

Cuddle

I'd rather have a cuddle
Than a video
I'd rather have a cuddle
Than anything I know
I'd rather have a cuddle
Than fish or chips
Or peas
A computer can be lovely
But
A cuddle's what I need.
Peter Dixon

Acknowledgements

My thanks go to all those who made this book possible. First of all, to the children, their parents and teachers who readily shared their experiences and positively discussed what could be done to include more time for play and so make things better. And as this went on, it was so heartening to see how the children gained confidence in their own abilities as they played and as they learned to initiate and share ideas to take their play forward. Teachers too recounted how really listening to the children and following their plans had enriched interactions and provided them with a plethora of ideas. This eased both their observations and their planning and enhanced the teacher–child relationship. This was because the children could see that their ideas were treated with respect.

A special thank-you to the teacher, poet and author Peter Dixon, who wrote the very generous Foreword to the book. He, with Vivien Paley, author of *You Can't Say You Can't Play*, among other gems, provided the inspiration for this book and it is wonderful to have such support.

Thank you to Lucy Wainwright at Routledge for being so patient and helpful and to my friends at Keystroke for the professional presentation of the text. Thank you to David Owen, who produces colourful flyers and markets the book.

And to you . . . those who read the books! I have met many of you at conferences and you have been kind enough to say hello and tell me how previous books have helped with your studies. This makes all the hard work so worthwhile. Thank you.

The aim of the book is to show how play is the most fantastic medium for learning for all children – with special needs or not – and to encourage all those who are involved with children to give them time and space to show and explain what they can do and what they would like to do. We have to recapture the joy of childhood for our children. We must have the knowledge to understand their development, the skill to plan appropriate teaching and the courage and belief, in Peter Dixon's words, 'to let them be'.

Introduction

All children must have time to play, and those with learning differences, who may find life more demanding and sometimes distressing, need even more of this special time – a time that should be free from the external demands that cause stress; a time when children can be free to play. For through this learning medium all aspects of their development can be enhanced. Play should happen in a setting that is happy – where there is no rush, no fear of failure – and where adults follow, then, if appropriate, develop the children's wishes, ideas and ideals. Through these kinds of experiences and interactions, children become confident, independent learners, increasingly able to use their imaginations, to care for others and to take safe risks. They learn to control their bodies and develop their intellectual, social and emotional abilities at this critically important developmental time. In so doing, they gain self-belief and so become motivated and enabled to do more and to learn more.

And yet there are those possibly well-meaning but in my view misguided people who would encroach on playtime and substitute activities where the children fail to meet adult standards and instead of exhilaration, feel only distress.

This said, there are many children, especially those with learning differences, who don't find playing easy. For them, playtimes can be fraught with difficulties. Perhaps they don't know what to do or perhaps other children won't let them play. But the answer is not to curtail playtime but to observe the children unobtrusively and discover how they can be helped. For play is the means by which children come to understand their world – it houses a life of communication and imagination as well as practice of the skills of daily living.

So, when there are difficulties, should adults just show children how to play? Can 'long out of practice oldies' really lead the way? Perhaps this sounds relatively straight-forward, but any intervention must be carefully gauged to begin where the children are and only suggest opportunities, resources and ideas commensurate with what they want to do, or else motivation and independence will be lost. So, careful observation based on understanding the different learning differences and the children's own plans must precede any decisions about how to intervene, or indeed whether to intervene at all.

This book tackles these issues, sharing with parents, teachers and other professionals details of different learning differences and ways to enhance their children's learning through play. But of course these same people will have to consider and amend the suggestions to suit each individual child. There is no one strategy that will suit them all. While this is challenging, it is also the essence of good teaching, and surely nothing can be more important, for it is to the young – *all* the young – that the future belongs.

Throughout this text, the term 'learning differences' is used alongside 'special needs', for replacing a negative model allows us to highlight the positive things all our children can achieve and reminds those who care that they must adapt their teaching to make it easier for children with learning differences to succeed, because, given understanding and tolerance, they certainly can!

Chapter 1

The ambience of the setting

A plea for time and calm

Please give me time to look and learn – to understand my day,
Please give me time to try things out before you show the way,
Please hold my hand and comfort me whenever things go wrong,
Please let me close my eyes awhile – the day can seem so long
Please understand that I am me and however much I try,
I cannot do what others do,
Please someone, tell me why?

Christine Macintyre

After working for many years with teachers, nursery nurses and teaching assistants who support children with learning differences, difficulties and disabilities, I penned this verse, hoping it might encapsulate children's feelings as they confront each day in nursery, at play group, with a childminder or at school. I need to explain two things. The first is why I find the pleas so important in structuring the best learning environment for young children, and the second is to show how, in the early years and beyond, this should be grounded in the optimum learning medium, play.

So why should these lines be relevant to the ways in which children learn and the ways in which we interact with children? Let's consider them in turn.

Please give me time to look and learn, to understand my day . . .

This first line reminds us that, while some children need a great deal of physical and psychological support, and others need less, all of them can manage a little more if they are just given time and space to plan their thoughts and their actions. This happens best when they are not harried and hassled by having to keep up with other children or when parents or teachers tell them – or imply, possibly by sighing, maybe by being brisk – that they are too slow or that they are wasting 'valuable' time! Many children just need a bit longer 'to understand their day', but when they do, they will realise that they have done well and their self-esteem will be enhanced. They will have learned and achieved! If children are not worried by 'doing things in time', they will be freed to concentrate on the task in hand. Hopefully that will be playing!

It is not surprising that many, perhaps even most, children need more time because the social nature of education means they are part of an ever-changing environment with different people, places and things. For those whose eyes need just a little longer to focus or who initially make inaccurate spatial judgements that need further planning or who see others threateningly close and need a moment to adjust their perceptions, having more time is an essential prerequisite to learning. And then there are the hypersensitive children who anticipate that noises and bright lights will prevent them from enjoying their day. Drums and maracas set out in the music area suggest there will be (to them) intolerable noise. There will also be children who are flustered and dismayed by any kind of change. The discovery that there is a new practitioner instead of their very favourite lady brings the fear that she might not know that they need help at the toilet or that they don't understand English too well. Is it any wonder that children can be overwhelmed by it all? The stress can become much worse if they have to add time pressure to their concerns.

Or perhaps more time is needed so that children can enjoy and act out their fantasies? Is this not a key part of being a child?

Listen to Gerda and Dino, Leah's 4-year-olds, who had been listening to the story of Icarus flying too near the sun. They came in from the garden with some autumn leaves clutched in their hands.

Gerda: Look at these poor leaves. They are all sad and crispy because the wind blew them up too near the sun and they got burnt.
Dino: And they went up into the clouds where the cloudberries live. The cloudberries pop when it rains and the leaves come down again but they aren't the same any more.
Gerda: The clouds are puffy and soft and swirly and the grey bits are the stems of the berries.
Dino: No, that's the seeds inside the berries – they are ready to pop out and be snowyberries. They are hard and hit you on the head and it's sore. Lots of snowyberries make a snowman.

Can anyone justify not giving the children time to use their imaginations and enjoy their fantasy life? Some of the other children picked up the rhythm of 'snowyberry' and soon a group were chanting variations midst lots of laughter when rainyberry, muddyberry, hailyberry and windyberry, even stinkyberry, were suggested. The children then acted out how the different berries would dance in the wind as they flew from the sun. Later another child mused, 'Sometimes in the winter the sky is all red and that's the leaves that stayed up there shining down. They didn't want to come down with the rain because they wanted to paint the sky.'

Whoever could have pre-planned a lesson on painting the sky? The children had so much fun and this led naturally to them asking about the colours in rainbows and considering different hues and tints. One group after hearing the story about the pot of gold that can be found at the end of the rainbow even made a stash of gold coins while the others painted a huge rainbow. Another child asked Leah if she had heard the story of the boy who searched for the house with gold windows. All of this developed from listening to the children and giving them time to fantasise a world much more colourful and lively than some of them had at home. And when little Lauren added, 'When I go to Heaven I'll see all the leaves and help to make them pretty because I'm good at painting', even the experienced teachers could only nod and blink away their tears.

So if the children's ideas are heard and treated with respect and developed and danced, their world can be richer than the adults' world. They are not limited by things having to be correct or better than someone else's. How lovely it can be when they are given time to follow their ideas through.

One child then asked if strawberries were made out of straw, and a more formal teacher-led lesson looking into the differences between growing and planting raspberries, blueberries, strawberries and cloudberries (these are grown in South Africa) naturally developed and led to other questions. 'Why are there no pinkberries or stinkyberries?' asked Grace. 'There must be pink berries,' replied Jake, 'because my Daddy drinks pink juice. He says it's medicine, but I know it's wine!' Then the name 'stinkyberries' raised the question of whether different berries had different smells, and a fun game of identifying raspberries, cherries and blackcurrants by their scents, then their tastes, was enjoyed.

But there was no doubt which part of the experience the children enjoyed most as requests 'to play the birling leaves again' met with claps and cheers! Their teacher, Leah, was enchanted to have supported the children in their fantasy play. She recorded that they had 'imagined new worlds' but in so doing felt the learning was diminished because her terse recording didn't really do justice to the children's imaginative story-making. 'It is so hard to record what makes learning experiences really special,' she explained, 'but how do you record the intensity, the laughter and the rhythm, the new ideas and the social learning in listening to others?' How do you show the smiles on all the faces, including my own? Furthermore, and very importantly, no one was left out. All the children could suggest a name or use the one someone else had suggested. And even the one or two children who couldn't say the words could join in, for they could make their hands and fingers dance.

Reflecting on the experience

Later Leah explained that she was so glad that she had experienced the children's fantasy play because she felt she had 'more than survived' letting the children take the lead in developing new ideas. She explained:

> I don't worry so much now because I know I can go with the flow, but it takes experience and confidence to do this. When the children are being imaginative, somehow they don't play up and be silly, they are engrossed in suggesting ideas.

She was also delighted that children with quite severe movement and planning difficulties joined in, even choosing to be whirlyberries when the reality was that their movement was quite restricted by cerebral palsy. She also was glad that one of the children on the autistic spectrum had joined in with the whirling actions. 'For once,' she exclaimed, 'Gordon didn't have to try to restrict his flapping and birling [spinning round]. It was all part of the fun.'

The total involvement meant that the learning was meaningful; there was something different, a whole new experience to be described at home and replayed at school. That would help the children retain the new learning in their memories.

But of course there are many other types of play that are important and they must be given time too if the curriculum is to be balanced and develop the myriad of skills and competences the children require.

Rote learning and meaningful learning

We also have to remember that there are many children who appear to be coping with the myriad of learning experiences they encounter in the day, but in truth are finding the pace difficult. They are likely to be resorting to rote learning rather than really understanding the meaning of what is being taught. Would they not also benefit from some extra time so that they could internalise more of the learning context and content at their own pace? If there was more time, they could explain any difficulties and have the teacher recap appropriately and so reinforce the content. Perhaps then they could remember more and store that learning in their memories so that they would have a comparative base when other, new learning came along? This process, called habituation, is particularly difficult for children with dyspraxia and dyslexia and other conditions where 'poor memorising' means that they have to tackle each task as a first-time try instead of starting from an informed base. Without recall, even carrying out basic skills can seem like learning to drive every time they are attempted!

The danger is that surface or rote learning can take over from meaningful learning, which, based in the child's own experience, is more readily remembered. Rote learning can promote instant recall and so is useful up to a point. For example, in the nursery it is useful to rote-learn routines, e.g. 'I get my pinny and then wash my hands before snack.' This aids memorising and remembering the sequence of events. Better still if there can be photos or other visual aids especially for children with Down's syndrome and others – for most children are visual learners, are they not?

So rote learning supports all kinds of instant recall, e.g. providing answers in quiz successes, remembering street names and train times and of course in helping children chant their times tables. It is also invaluable for helping children to acquire the skills of daily living, e.g. safely carrying and using scissors, pouring hot liquid, hammering nails and chiselling wood.

When children don't understand safety issues or refuse to comply or do not understand the implications of actions, then using 'rules' and demonstrations to show the most efficient way makes sense. It is too dangerous to let them discover ways for themselves. Many children on the autistic spectrum (see Appendix 3) benefit from ABA therapy (applied behaviour analysis), where everyday tasks are broken down into components that match the child's competence and these parts are practised separately, and then combined till the skill is achieved. Then they gain a reward. This promotes competent behaviour without the need for the children to rationalise or problem-solve but it does build up a skill base so that children can safely do more things for themselves. But skills in isolation, i.e. taken out of context, can lack meaning. Many children on the autistic spectrum find it particularly difficult if not impossible to attach meaning, a process that is intuitive in most children. Charlotte Moore (2004) tells of her son Sam, who had autism. He had a favourite soft toy, as many neurotypical children do, 'but the toy was a comforter, not a friend, he never gave it a name or a personality'. So his playing experience was severely restricted by his condition. This, i.e. how children use their toys, could provide a key focus for observation for practitioners in an early years setting.

Attaching meaning to experience

But real learning comes when attached meaning turns an isolated experience into a personalised 'whole'. Think of a child receiving a birthday gift. Even young children soon recognise that the giver has chosen something with care and that feelings will be hurt if it is not received graciously. For them, remembering the exchange will symbolise a whole social experience and will be used as a basis for understanding the giving and receiving that is part of everyday living. But children who have a disjointed sense of reality may be dismayed that the parcel was wrapped up at all and may even be dismayed by the torn-off paper, for some attribute feelings to inanimate objects.

Transfer of learning

Memorising helps the transfer of learning from one experience to another. If the teacher could point out similarities between what the children do and how this is similar to other people's experience, transfer would be helped. So after the children have fetched their aprons for painting, the teacher could explain that 'Nurses at the hospital wear aprons too to save spreading germs and to keep their uniforms clean – can you think of other people who do this?' It is important that this transfer is explained because many children with learning differences will not make connections like this.

I have always been entranced by Rush's (1997) story. She explained:

> After I had taught Emma to swim at school, she asked me. 'Now can you come and teach me to swim in my pool at home?' I hadn't thought to explain that her new skill could transfer to swimming in other pools or the sea. I was taken aback!

And, on reflection, Emma's teacher, Ann, explained:

> I didn't realise how much I was taking the children's ability to transfer for granted. Now I know that if this doesn't happen intuitively, there have to be explanations that extend and reinforce the detail of how transfer can occur. Only then can one learning experience be recalled and used again to ease further learning.

If there was more time, she asked, 'Might we not discover much more about how different children learn and how to support those who find it difficult?' And that is so true.

So as Paley (2005: 73) explains: '"B" is for Bear – a good thing to know, but (whenever possible) the child must also know what it is like to be the father bear and how bears might get across a poison river.' She is acknowledging the usefulness of rote learning but emphasising the importance of fantasy play in developing children's imaginations. In many homes and even in some schools, computer games have displaced free, imaginative play. So it is important that in settings, fantasy play readdresses the richer, more personal moments when children enjoy being imaginative. Rote learning can provide children with stability, but only fantasy play can foster creativity and give them the wings to fly beyond wherever their teachers are. Or perhaps if they both enter the fantasy world they can travel together.

> **Key considerations**
>
> Reduce the number of things children have to achieve. Listen to the children and let them take the lead in fantasy play. Help them to see the links between achieving one skill and using it again in another situation. Above all, give the children time and space to learn.

One wonderful and really unanticipated finding emerged from Paley's (2005) research to find how effective giving more time was. That was:

> The children were kinder to one another, more 'less able' children were encouraged to join in because there was time to explain and everyone could relax and enjoy because there were no wrong answers – and the atmosphere in the setting was noticeably calmer.

How wonderful is that? Surely this must give all educators pause for thought and encourage them in the journey to follow and so understand their children.

The second line of the poem says:

Please give me time to try things out before you show the way

This line, focussing on intervention, was written to highlight the fact that many practitioners are so anxious to support their children that they jump in to make suggestions or do tasks for the children that, with time, the children could accomplish for themselves. Very often, the interventions are made so that the children achieve externally set curriculum goals – some inappropriate in my view – and so get ticks in boxes. Or interventions may be made so that the children with learning differences don't appear to lag behind their peers.

When I ask teachers, 'Do you ever feel when you intervene, i.e. go in and make suggestions when children are busily occupied or even when they are just standing and staring, that you are intruding and spoiling the development of their play?' Invariably they answer 'Yes', even 'Yes, all the time!' But then they go on to explain why. 'We feel conditioned to get in there and help, it's what we do – it's what we are paid for.' This is so understandable, for it is the hardest thing to wait and keep back, especially when you, as the more knowing adult, have a good idea as to how the children might proceed or when you feel that over-the-shoulder expectations are that you 'move in and teach'. It is so hard to keep back! However, intervening too soon can take away the children's motivation to plan and do things for themselves. They then wait for further instructions and this denies them the satisfaction of achievement, following through their own ideas and becoming independent learners. Of course this does not mean that practitioners adopt a *laissez-faire* attitude and do nothing. This is a time to observe and develop eyes that can see what is really happening and to plan future learning possibilities on the basis of that.

For there will be time for structured teaching in the day – of course there will. This is vitally important. But before that, teachers have to 'set aside political goals and find out what the needs of children really are' (Trevarthen 1977). The timing, the type and the amount of intervention are critically important, but such 'when do I intervene, when do I stay back and what do I do?' decisions are far from easy.

Jake, a newly qualified practitioner, was clearly mystified by this approach. When I suggested he stay back and observe, he asked, 'How long do we have to wait?' and the answer, 'Watch the children and find the moment when they have switched off and have no more to offer before you intervene', really didn't convince him that this was a good strategy! Luckily, in the background some more experienced practitioners were nodding that that is what they tried to do.

And, of course, intervention doesn't mean totally taking over. It could mean just placing a toy in the sand and waiting to see if this stimulated further thinking or perhaps placing scissors alongside a drawing, because that could suggest (non-verbally) that cutting out could enhance the craft.

Jake explained that he had tried to do that. He had told Aaron to make his drawing into a calendar and together they had pasted sequins on the front and, to quote Jake, had produced a 'really pleasing result'. Sadly, at going home time, Jake was devastated when he heard Aaron tell his mum, 'Here's something Jake made. It's nice but I wanted to make a Get Well card for Granny. Why would she want a calendar?'

Listen to Brooklyn, who is a nursery nurse working with 3- and 4-year-olds. She paints a realistic picture that shows how difficult it is to achieve this balance between waiting (observing) and acting. She explains:

> It's just so much easier just to do things for the children or tell them what to do, otherwise we'd never get done. Some of the children will daydream and wander around watching what everyone else is doing or they'll just be getting involved when it's time to move on to something else or they'll just waste time. If we don't chivvy them along we'll have dough all over the tables and water on the floor. The place would look a mess and we'd not be able to record what they had achieved. How could we keep our records up to date? There is so much pressure to put ticks in boxes nowadays!

Both Brooklyn and Jake are experiencing the conflict that exists between observing the children to build a curriculum on their needs, giving them time to watch other children and learn from their example, as against 'simply getting things done' to meet the demands of some external policy or to enable assessment boxes to be ticked. It is difficult to make decisions like these; getting the balance is hard, but once adults take the lead through intervening too soon or inappropriately, then the children often wait to follow their instructions. Then cries of 'What will I do now?' supplant following their own thoughts and plans, for in the children's eyes at least, adults know best!

Grace has responsibility for children with learning differences in a children's centre. She explains that one of her children, Carla, age 5, has cerebral palsy (see Appendix 4) and another child, 4-year-old Darrel, has Down's syndrome (see Appendix 1). She explains:

> When I met Carla and Darrel, I was so afraid that they would get upset that I did far too much for them. It was so distressing to see them struggle with tasks the other children do easily. Carla, who has athetoid cerebral palsy, has a weakness

right down one side of her body and her muscles occasionally go into spasm so that she finds control difficult. She has a special chair to support her at table, but often she spends so long trying to feed herself that her meal is cold and usually it's spilled all down her front. Then she wipes her hands in it all. I really didn't see the point of letting her try by herself and getting into this mess till one day a spoonful went right in where it was supposed to go and her eyes lit up and she looked around to make sure we saw and praised her. That was just magic, yet I could so easily have deprived her of that moment and of the motivation that success gave her to keep trying. Cool food was really a small price to pay for that achievement. So now I try to judge when she might be successful and when she's really over-whelmed and getting tired and frustrated before I do things for her.

With Darrel, it's a different story. He is much less compliant. When he doesn't get his own way he lies on the floor and shrieks and that upsets me so I give in and don't establish any boundaries. If I ignore the shrieking, even stepping over him when he lies on the floor, he starts to kick and bite and some of the children are frightened. Although he's not tall, he's sturdy and strong. His mum says that when he was younger he was so happy and willing to please, but since he came to nursery, he behaves badly at home too. I wondered if she thought this was my fault!

The other children know Darrel is different, but they also anticipate how he will react and sometimes they hand over their toys even before he asks. They'll do anything to placate him and save an outburst. Maybe we've got to ignore his disability and treat him like any other child? This is a different kind of intervention, but he needs to calm down. How can we help him to settle? [See Appendix 1 for explanations of Down's syndrome.]

Intervention takes on a totally different meaning when children are distressed or endangered by another child. Then steps to keep all of them safe have to have top priority. Children with Down's syndrome generally do not have behavioural diffi-culties, but their developmental delay may mean that they are experiencing all the frustrations and outbursts of the terrible twos, two years later when they are 4. And of course children who have been overly sheltered may be experiencing sharing for the first time and need time and experience and explanations to learn that other children have needs and rights too.

So if Darrel is safe and not hurting anyone, then ignoring poor behaviour and 'catching him being good' is the first step, but physical restraint may have to be used if danger to himself or other children is possible. His Mum has to be made aware of what restraint entails and preferably agree that this is the best way.

Key consideration

Try to be aware of how intervention cuts into children's planning, and when this happens – and it will – consider other ways you could have acted or visualise what might have happened if you had watched and waited instead. Perhaps you only needed to say 'AH'?

Interaction practice: Find six ways of saying 'AAHH'. Ask a friend, 'What does this AAhh mean?' See Table 1.1.

Table 1.1 Six meanings of 'Aahh'

Aahh	Meaning	Mode
Aahhh	This work is coming on nicely; keep going	Say it softly and almost privately
AAAhhh	What a lovely surprise!	Let other children hear the positive news
AAAAAh	Wow, that is frightening! What can we do?	Use this as a spur to make other children give suggestions
AHHHHH	That is really sad. What can we do to make it better?	Say the first part gently and quietly but the second part more positively
AA – HA	Well, whatever next? That looks like fun!	Convey surprise and pleasant anticipation
AAAAA	Haven't you/we done well?	Convey real pleasure in the achievement

NB. Remember that even this gentle intervention may appear meaningless or intrusive to children who are on the autistic spectrum. This is because they will be unlikely to be looking for external approval or they will not understand the differences in intonation. Any interruptions may disrupt their concentration without them understanding the tenor of sounds or words that are meant to convey encouragement or the teacher's (dis)pleasure. For these children, praise can be confusing. It is not always welcome!

The third line of the poem asks:

Please hold my hand and comfort me whenever things go wrong

Admittedly, this plea flies in the face of health and safety advice that tells practitioners not to touch children. But children who find life perplexing, at times very difficult, even painful and frightening, need the reassurance of being held and soothed. In fact, I would attest that all children benefit from being touched appropriately and learning how to touch/comfort others. Surely this is the basis of social and emotional development? A hug or even a sympathetic hand on the shoulder can so easily convey empathy when words are inadequate or difficult to find. What is the alternative? That children stay isolated when they are hurt? Surely not?

The poem also considers the stresses and pressures that children face each day as they leave a busy home and venture into a new environment. It begs adults to see their setting through the children's eyes and note anything that could inadvertently cause anxiety or even anguish to a hypersensitive child. Things that are taken for granted by adults (e.g. that locks on the door are to keep the children safe, not to keep ogres out) can stimulate fears. Some things practitioners have been advised to do, e.g. mounting the children's work on several layers of coloured paper and laminating the whole (so that the light reflects into children's sensitive eyes) is so unnecessary and wasteful, and the effect can cause real distress. Even having a wealth of highly coloured resources spread around making routes and pathways confusing can jar the senses. All of these potentials have to be re-evaluated in the light of the support needs of children who are in the setting.

Then there is the line that practitioners may wish had been written for them:

Please let me close my eyes awhile – the day can seem so long . . .

How comforting it is for children to know that it is all right to shut the world out for a while. And who knows what children are thinking as they 'escape' into realms of fantasy? Even if they are not thinking about anything, even if they are having a nap, they are recharging their batteries, and this is so important for children whose lives are more fraught with anxiety than their peers'. A few moments to regain calm can give children who have control issues, e.g. ADHD (attention deficit hyperactivity disorder, see Appendix 2), time to settle and reduce their urges to move or shout out. Often children can explain when they feel sensations of panic building up. If they know they will be able to have some quiet time whenever they need it, this can relieve so much stress. Sensory overload can be avoided if there is time just 'to be'.

And beyond this group, there are children who are simply tired. Young children have many coughs and colds because their developing immune systems may not be robust, so sleep patterns are disturbed. Parents may also give in to pleas to stay up late to watch television or play computer games just to have some quality time together. But children's minds shouldn't be constantly stimulated with no respite. The concept of the power nap is intriguing, for surely it is better to shut off for a while than struggle and lose the motivation to learn?

Now listen to Jenny, a nursery nurse who is anxious about her 3-year-olds:

I wonder who thought up the notion that 3-year-olds come to nursery in the afternoon while 4-year-olds have the morning session? Certainly some of them cope but I have other children who appear asleep on their feet. One young boy looks forward to coming all morning – he has to be up and around early to get his older brother to school – and by the time he comes to nursery, all he is able to do is to creep into the bed in the house corner and fall asleep. On one or two occasions his mum has had to carry him out to the car, still sleeping. No one who understands children made this master plan!

But of course the issue of tiredness goes beyond the 3-year-olds. Many pasty-faced children who have not had sufficient sleep appear in school each day and some have sleep apnoea as part of their learning difference (SEN).

There are also children who find it very difficult to be still and pay attention, for sitting still and standing still are the hardest movements of all. Some children with balance difficulties have to keep moving so that their proprioceptors, i.e. the nerve endings in the muscles, joints and skin, relay positional information to tell them where they are in space. If their proprioceptors don't work efficiently, then the children have to concentrate hard to sustain their balance and their attention towards other learning is impaired.

Key considerations

Take time to think like a child. Visualise the day as a time line with highs and lows showing peaks and troughs of activity. Is there a balance? How could this balance be achieved? Do children know it's all right to do nothing for a while? Could you explain something like this or how would you convey this idea to your children?

The penultimate lines say,

Please understand that I am me and however much I try, I cannot do what others do . . .

How dreadful it must be for children to feel inadequate day after day when they discover they cannot do what others do. Children do not appreciate that what they are being asked to do may well be inappropriate for their stage of development. They think that inability to meet the demands of the day is their fault. When the children develop self-awareness, practitioners must strive to prevent them self-evaluating as failures, for who can keep motivated to learn when difficulties constantly prevent success? Of course, children on the autistic spectrum may not be concerned at all. They won't envy others' prowess or feel guilty that they cannot compete. They have many problems, but generally can be self-sufficient, not ambitious to meet external demands or striving to be 'top dog' as many children are – or are pressured to be.

As the numbers of children with a whole range of special educational needs conditions are increasing rapidly (Keen and Ward explain that there is an 80 per cent increase in numbers of children presenting for assessment since 2001) and more and more severe conditions such as autism are common, an increasing number of children will require specific individualised educational programmes. In 2007, the National Autistic Society had 125,000 children in the UK recorded on their lists, and most named support groups, e.g. the Dyspraxia Foundation, report large increases too. Teachers also share their concerns about the number of children who have communication, movement and intellectual difficulties. But why should this be? Paley (2005) has an interesting and valid response. She claims that when we meet children we no longer ask, 'Who are you?', but instead instinctively frame the (unspoken) question, 'How can we fix you?' Again this is a question of balance between intervening too soon when the process of maturation may alleviate concerns and leaving intervention too late so that the critical learning times are missed and remediation is more difficult. But it is never too late; for some children, progress will be slow but it does happen and if children ask, they must be reassured that this is the case.

This kind of concern, i.e. as professionals we are seeing the deficits (how can we fix you?) rather than the children (who are you?), led to the change of name from 'learning difficulties' to 'learning differences', the idea being that practitioners would identify the way each child learned most easily and change their planning and teaching to match. This meant that children with gifts and talents could also come into this 'learning differences' spectrum. While this, in my view, is an excellent step forward, there is no doubt that the differences children show usually lead to difficulties in meeting the standard curricular goals. Neihart (2003) has some thought-provoking advice that should have an impact on practice. For while many professionals spotting a learning difference immediately focus on that, with the aim of helping the child catch up, she says, 'NO!' She worries that concentrating on what is seen as a deficit will undermine the children's self-esteem – for at this age the children make a global appraisal of 'self-worth'. She asks teachers to 'concentrate on the things the children do well while paying attention to the things they find difficult'. In this way, she hopes that difficulties will be kept in proportion and not outweigh the children's strengths or diminish their self-esteem.

Key consideration

Before trying to make the match, practitioners should have time to understand the different conditions children have. Only then can they adapt their input appropriately. (See the Appendices for introductory descriptions of different learning differences/difficulties/disabilities.)

The last line of the poem is:

> Please someone, tell me why?

This last line raises the issue of sharing information with the children themselves and their peer group. The question of giving very young children a label is one fraught with difficulties and different opinions. Some parents worry that if their child has a label, 'teachers will just see the condition and not the child and make wrong assumptions about what he can and can't do'. Kim's dad was adamant that giving young children labels was wrong. Mark's mum, Elaine, agreed (Mark, aged 6, has ADHD), and explained her fears:

> I'm afraid that his teachers will heed what 'someone says' or 'what a book says' rather than asking me about my child's level of difficulty and above all what his strengths are. If he has a problem, they might just assume nothing can be done.

Many other parents fear that practitioners' expectations will be lowered if a specific condition is mentioned. 'I know that the teachers won't stop teaching, they assure me that my child has a right to an equal amount of their time,' explained the mum of a 4-year-old who had been told he had developmental delay across the board, 'but I worry that they won't extend his learning; they'll not stretch him. And he knows very well how to get out of things he doesn't want to do.' With a wry smile she explained, 'Having a disability doesn't turn him into an angel!'

However, there is the other side of the coin. Young people such as Luke Jackson (2002), who has Asperger's syndrome, tell professionals that

> It is your duty to tell children what is wrong because then they can understand; they don't spend their lives worrying it is something worse and they can

participate in action plans to improve their lot. Above all, they find out that it's not their fault and that takes away feelings of letting the family down.

An experienced head teacher of a school for children with autistic spectrum conditions agrees, claiming that it is not good to let the children remain ignorant of their condition, because if they don't know what is wrong and are not reassured that their condition is something they were born with, then they can come to believe that they are bad. However, this decision of course would depend on the parents' wishes, the child's preference and perhaps on the kind or level of learning difference the child had. Moreover, the other children can learn to empathise more easily if they understand what is wrong and that the child is not being deliberately naughty or tiresome. It is the fear of not knowing the extent of the problem or how the affected child will react that can make the other children keep away. Sometimes, as no one has explained otherwise, they fear they will catch whatever the disability is. 'I knew my writing was the worst in the school,' explained Aaron, an intelligent, articulate 10-year-old with dyspraxia. The others told me I had a disease and that I shouldn't come to their school.' How dreadful is that?

So we have to see each and every child as one with a 'learning difference', and with the parents' permission and in line with the school policy, be able to recognise and explain a child's difficulties in a practical no-fuss, acceptingly positive way and devise a curriculum focussing on their strengths. Chapter 2 shows that this can best be done through a curriculum based on play.

Chapter 2

The essence of play
Supporting children who find it difficult to play

Guess what, I am a special child,
I have a special Mum,
School makes me work hard all day long,
There's not much time for fun.
It will be worth it, I've been told,
One day I will be glad,
But it's today and I am young,
The pressure drives me mad.
My truly precious childhood years,
The best days so they say,
Spent catching up with boring stuff?
Please teacher, let me play!
For playing gives me so much joy,
I'm best at that, you see.
Why must I sit and learn strange things
That do not interest me?
Just let me play, that's how I'll learn
And then I'll make you proud.
I'll run and swim and learn to sing
And fly beyond the clouds!

Christine Macintyre

This chapter considers and takes a new look at three key questions. They are:

1   What is play and why is this the best learning medium for children, especially those who find some/many things difficult?
2   Why should some children find it difficult to play?
3   What strategies will help children to play together?

Let's begin by asking question 1, 'What is play?' and discover its benefits, particularly for children with learning differences, difficulties and disabilities.

Over the years, many people have attempted to define play and put forward the idea that 'Play is a child's work' and that children don't differentiate between work and play. While that is so for the younger ones, I'm sure that by age 4 or 5, they do! Suddenly tasks like drying dishes, especially at home, are things to be avoided! And yet they have many years left when play is so important. In fact, it is salutary to ask if we, as adults, ever want to stop playing.

Other professionals claim that the ethereal and pervasive nature of children's play means that it doesn't make sense to try to pin it down, and many teachers attempting to frame a comprehensive description would probably agree. One enchanting try by Reilly (1974) explains that trying to describe play 'is like trying to catch the wind in a paper bag', and many experienced and committed early years educators will nod and smile! However, in this age of accountability and checklists, describing the core of the early years curriculum must be more tangible, so that people not actually able to observe children and analyse what they do as they play and those who are asked to *justify* what children are learning in their setting have the words so to do. This is vitally important, else inroads will be made by those who mistakenly believe that formal 'work' should replace time to play.

These people have not understood Vygotsky (1978) when he showed that 'in play, a child stands taller than himself, above his age and ordinary behaviour', nor even appreciated the negative effects of stress that occurs when children are pushed beyond their comfort/maturational zone (Palmer 2006). These children may well replace meaningful learning that endures with rote learning that provides instant recall but, in excluding meaning, hinders the transfer of learning that is at the root of intelligent behaviour. In my view, those who over-promote its use are asking children to build their house upon the sand.

For many years my favourite quotation came from Susan Isaacs, who as long ago as 1933 explained that 'Play is a child's life and the means by which he comes to understand the world around him.' She was, in effect, saying that nothing could be more important to children than learning the mores of their own culture and the ways of those who play a part in their community. But in the light of Paley's (2005) convincing endorsement of fantasy/imaginative play, I wonder if that aspect of play has not been underplayed, even omitted from Isaacs' definition? Certainly for children who do not or cannot use their imaginations to picture a world that is beyond them rather than around them, this would encompass the skills they required, but would it cover the competences children use when they visualise 'painting the sky' (see Chapter 1)? Perhaps the part imagination plays needs to be spelled out? Can it really form a bridge between fantasy and reality? What do you think?

For the moment, let's stay with Isaacs. In the first part of her description, 'Play is a child's life . . .', she is showing that play is everything a very young child does. So, play may involve hard physical work, and that requires children to have well-developed movement abilities.

Developing motor competence within play

Think of the satisfaction in building large blocks or trundling tyres and the strengthening effect on young muscles and limbs (see Figures 2.1 and 2.2). To be able to do these things children need balance, coordination and control and they must be able to make complex judgements about where and when and how to move themselves and their resources.

Very many children with learning differences find movement tasks really problematic. This goes well beyond dyspraxia, for children with dyslexia, dyscalculia and dysgraphia as well as those on the autistic spectrum are likely to have movement problems too. In fact, movement difficulties can often be the very first sign that something

Figure 2.1 Building bricks. This still requires perception of pattern, spatial awareness and the ability to let go in a controlled way.

Figure 2.2 Trundling a tyre. This requires strength, a sense of timing, balance and coordination.

is amiss. It is vital that the basic movement skills are acquired as near the 'right time' as possible because so many other skills, e.g. speaking, toilet training, getting dressed, depend on muscular control and several body parts working together. Poor muscle tone (hypotonia), which hampers coordination and balance, is also evident in children with Down's syndrome and, of course, cerebral palsy. Some of the children later found to have autism also are likely to have a strange gait, as their steps lack fluency. One explanation is that these children 'lack a sense of central coherence' – they 'have rather a disjointed feel of their own bodies'. Carter (2004) clarifies this by describing a lady with autism who would feel something touching her arm and, on looking down, being surprised that it was her other hand. With young children, observers can be perplexed by seeing children who walk with a strange gait, almost as if their legs were being dragged along trying to catch up with the top half of their bodies. Could this segregated feeling be a cause?

Milestones of motor development from 2 to 6

Please note that these norms (i.e. statistics derived from observation of hundreds of same-age children) are only rough guides. Some children will walk at 7 months, others at 18 months, and both are absolutely fine. Differences are influenced by the children's body build, their temperament and their intrinsic motivation. Also important are the number of opportunities the children have and the presence of role models. However, severe delay should always be investigated.

There is an inbuilt developmental sequence – and this is the same for every child in every culture (Trevarthen 1977). Children will intuitively move to the next stage when they are ready, i.e. when they have the muscular and neurological development to do so (see Table 2.1). This is the concept of 'readiness', and teachers and parents should not try to push children when they are not ready to tackle the next stage. As Palmer (2006) explains, 'Development happens in biological time.' Adults have to trust children to know when they can progress. Children with learning differences may stay a little longer and need more support and praise at each stage, but they will progress. Sometimes after a long period of trying, things happen. How good is that?

It used to be considered that if children's gross motor skills (crawling, walking, running, jumping, and using combined patterns) developed well, then their fine motor skills would follow on naturally and be trouble-free. Now we recognise that the developmental pathways are different, so it is important to observe skills such as threading to find whether hand strength and coordination are allowing age-related skills such as tracking and aiming to develop. This is particularly important if delay is suspected.

Two key movement competences are crawling and threading (a form of aiming that uses the pincer grip, because inability to do these has far-reaching consequences for learning).

Crawling

Crawling is a key motor skill that should be practised every day! The crawling pattern is the same as that used in climbing. In the early years settings it is usually relatively easy to set up opportunities for crawling – under tables, round skittles, even up stairs. This pattern should demonstrate the cross-lateral pattern as seen in the photos of Amy

Table 2.1 Age-related patterns of motor development

Age	Locomotor skills	Non-locomotor skills	Manipulative skills
3 months	Can roll over from back to front	Plays with hands as first toy	Can reach and grasp if given time; cannot release object/let go
4 months	Rolls over and pushes up, strengthening shoulders	Hands and toes go to mouth	Passes object from hand to hand but if it drops, finds it hard to retrieve
6 months +	Attempts to move from the spot with some sense of purpose	Sits, for moments, unsupported. Without support, tends to fall backwards due to heavy head	Will use two objects together, e.g. banging toys together; copies adults
7–10 months	Crawls. Check that the action is cross-lateral, i.e. one hand forward then the opposite foot	Claps hands; waves 'bye-bye' to order	
12 months	Pulls self up and walks round furniture Walks unaided	Scribbling; 'answers' toy telephone	Beginning to feed independently if messily! Will pull toy truck and rock doll
12–18 months	Walks, and crawls if that is faster	Plays games such as peek-a-boo. Enjoys repetition, e.g. 'Round and round the garden'	
18–24 months	Runs (20 mo), walks well (24 mo); climbs stairs with both feet on each step	Pushes and pulls boxes or wheeled toys; unscrews lid on a jar. Uses two hands at the midline of the body to do different things	Uses either hand indiscriminately; no hand preference yet; stacks 4 to 6 blocks; turns pages one at a time; picks things up without overbalancing
2–3 years	Runs easily; climbs up and down furniture unaided	Hauls and shoves big toys around obstacles. Begins to estimate distances between objects	Picks up small objects (e.g. Cheerios); throws small ball forward while standing. Little sense of transference of weight to aid propulsion
3–4 years	Walks up stairs one foot per step; may walk on tiptoe but can put heels down to walk steadily. Runs and jumps as a sequence but overbalances easily	Pedals and steers a tricycle; walks in any direction pulling a big toy; rotates body when throwing but still only uses one arm	Catches large ball between outstretched arms; cuts paper with scissors; threads beads but not needle
4–5 years	Walks up and down stairs one foot per step; stands, runs, jumps and walks well	Boys show mature throwing action. Girls especially use pens well for writing, and boys emergent writing	Strikes ball with bat; kicks and catches ball; builds mini games with friends
5–6 years	Skips on alternate feet; walks a thin line; slides, swings; can ride a bike	Uses combined skills with ease, e.g. kicking a ball on the run; climbs with control. Lands safely from a height	Plays ball games quite well; threads needle and sews stitches

Figure 2.3 Amy's crawling ability shows strength, balance and cross-lateral coordination

crawling and Andrew climbing the bars (Figures 2.3 and 2.4). This shows one hand going forward followed by the opposite foot. It is vital to observe that children are not crawling using a homolateral pattern, i.e. the hand and foot on the same side moving at the same time, or bum-shuffling. This is because it is only the cross-lateral pattern that aids coordination at the midline of the body, a skill that is needed in most everyday home tasks such as using a knife and fork, or getting dressed, and in nursery activities, e.g. in cutting, hammering and gardening. Much later, 'real writing' can be very difficult if the cross-lateral pattern has not been achieved.

If children seem reluctant to try to crawl, it may be best to begin with rolling over from lying on the back onto the front. This first step encourages the baby or child to push up to look outwards. This can be difficult because of the weight of the head, but even short moments of trying strengthen muscles and take the possibility of crawling one step nearer. Dangling a toy just out of reach can help the child's motivation, but 'readiness' is paramount here. Crawling is very complex for those who do not do it naturally. These children may have a retained primitive reflex (the ATNR, asymmetric tonic neck reflex) and need specific practices to help wash it away (Goddard Blythe 2005).

Figure 2.4 Andrew shows the cross-lateral pattern in climbing. This sophisticated pattern needs strength and sequencing skills to cope with the widely spaced bars.

Threading

Threading is another complex fine motor task. It involves aiming using the pincer grip. If children find this very difficult, their eyes may not be working together due to poor muscle tone, and specialist help from an optician may be required. Children with Down's syndrome, who often have just one palmar crease, may find difficulty in grasping the lace or whatever is to be threaded, and so altering the resource, e.g. using a straw or firm piece of wood, can help.

All the basic motor milestones can be analysed in this way and support in terms of changing the resources or simplifying the pattern can pay huge dividends in terms of success the children can feel and see. This means that their self-esteem will be enhanced – an essential step in supporting children with learning differences (see Chapter 5).

NB. It is important to practise skills in a real context, i.e. as children play. Children do not learn by practising skills for the sake of it; they learn best when they see the purpose and feel the essence of what they are trying to do.

Developing social competence within play

Think of being able to take on different characters in role-play scenarios (Table 2.5) and the social and emotional communication/learning that brings (Figure 2.5). As children act out being mummy or daddy or indeed any character they choose, they are taking the first steps in developing a theory of mind (Baron-Cohen 1991), i.e. they are learning to appreciate how another person is thinking or feeling as they carry out their tasks and relate to others doing theirs. This is very necessary if they are to develop empathy and altruism, i.e. the attributes that underlie caring for others and willingly sharing resources and experiences.

Children on the autistic spectrum, even the most intellectually bright ones, have severe limitations in this aspect of their development. Of course they do think and feel emotions but these are 'made different' by the children being unable to appreciate the implications of their actions on others, i.e. their lack of a theory of mind. This is also influenced by the fact that deep in their brains, the amygdala, i.e. one of the areas concerned with negative emotions, functions differently (Carter 2004). So the children have to rote-learn ideas about turn taking and sharing rather than naturally absorbing them from gauging the reactions of others and watching what they do. This may take a very long time and require ABA therapy. On the other hand, many children with Down's syndrome seem naturally sociable and are skilled at role play.

Arron (2006) suggests that there is a gene effect that supports this aspect of their development, and this gives them a real advantage as people warm to their smile. This happens despite the children generally having lower intelligence scores than other children with learning differences. However, this claim is countered by Wishart (2006), who explains that the popular notion that 'children with Down's syndrome are *always* happy and sociable is a myth'. Perhaps those children who don't smile have not been the recipients of the comforting interactions that children with easily recognisable disabilities often meet? In such cases, the environmental effects, i.e. of nurture, would overcome the genetic effects of nature. Or perhaps some children are more aware of their limitations? Or perhaps the gene effect is selective, not supporting all children who have Down's syndrome? It is so difficult to identify accurately the learning potential within play when children bring their own aptitudes, attitudes and abilities to the scene.

Figure 2.5 Preparing for a tea party. Spreading needs an accurate assessment of the strength required, the ability to make both hands work together at the middle of the body, and a well-developed sense of balance.

What kind of learning is developed by different play scenarios?

Well, to take just one example, think of the intensive concentration needed to pour water down narrow funnels to observe the effect of that action on the water already in the tray.

Think first of the cognitive or intellectual problems the children are solving, e.g. how fast should I pour and how do I make ripples on the water? Perhaps the water will make waves and the faster the flow, the higher the waves will be? Or how high do the waves need to be to cause the floating toy to move? Play activities like these are mini-experiments that relate to scientific learning about volume and flow, capacity and the effect of one action on another.

And as the play develops, social learning is fostered too because one child needs another to hold the tubes and funnels at the correct height and they need to communicate and cooperate to produce different effects in the water tray.

Then picture children setting a table and think of the mathematical correspondence they need to appreciate the correct numbers of cups and cutlery needed for 'guests'. There might also be discussions about food and the recipe needed to make it. And what about the aesthetic appreciation of matching colours and patterns as they make their table attractive and pleasant to behold? These are important gains too. So in play, intellectual learning goes far beyond the children's ability to count to ten and write their name.

Figure 2.6 Rob's scowl shows what he thinks of this activity!

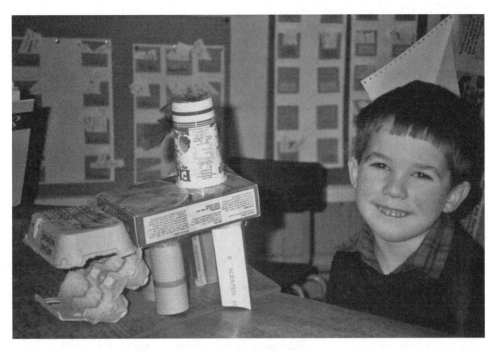

Figure 2.7 Glyn's smile shows how delighted he is with his dragon

Indeed, this writing practice is unsuitable for many little boys, because the gender difference in development means that the language centre tends to develop, i.e. be myelinated, slightly later, making formal writing at an early age an inappropriate demand (Figure 2.6). However, boys are ahead in spatial decision-making and making models, as Glyn shows when he chooses to make a 'scaredy dragon' (Figure 2.7).

Development of speech through play – a cognitive, motor, social and emotional achievement!

Each child's acquisition and comprehension of speech is an important basis for their all-round development. To help plot progress, there are norms for the acquisition of speech too (Table 2.2).

At each stage it is critically important to differentiate between poor articulation and lack of comprehension. Surprising poor articulation, given the child's obvious ability to understand and evaluate spoken interactions, can be caused by lack of tone in the muscles of the speech apparatus, i.e. the lips, tongue and soft palate. A small number of children may have (s)elective mutism, finding it impossible to speak in unfamiliar places. These children can speak coherently and readily in the security of their home but, as Daniel explains, 'When I try to speak at school, a huge lump in my throat prevents sounds coming out.' A play environment where there is no time constraint and the children can follow their own pursuits is surely the one to instil confidence and the best place to gain confidence. Then the lump can go away!

Table 2.2 A developmental plan for speaking

Age	Words	Stories	Activities
5 years	Clear articulation Compound phrases	Can retell a story; suggest new ideas Can sequence three pictures Uses pronouns correctly now	Can empathise with others' feelings; understands rules and routines
4 years	Seeks explanations Asks 'When? 'Why?' Can visualise events elsewhere	Enjoys repetition and contributing known phrases to stories	Can role-play Can understand characterisation
3 years	Uses sentences of 4–5 words Complex use of words	Will listen, adapt and recast sentences	Joins in songs and rhymes Beats rhythms
2 years	Huge increase in vocabulary – the naming explosion Links two words, e.g. 'love you', 'go away' Assertions such as 'NO' clearly announced	Follows stories – recognises favourite characters and routines Gesture and body language combined, i.e. holophrases Communication strategies used, e.g. motherese (higher-pitched simplified language).	Asserts independence – tantrums Telegraphic speech, i.e. uses only essential words, e.g. 'I going'
I year	Monosyllabic babbling: da, da, da Understanding evident from facial expression and gestures	Understands simple instructions, e.g. 'come here' Can convey wishes through gestures Understands 50 words; makes own words for wants Words learned slowly at this pre-linguistic stage	Enjoys peep-bo (the basis of turn-taking) Memory and a sense of self are developing

From this brief introduction to the value of play, have I convinced you that the range of abilities and skills involved in 'just playing' can enhance every aspect of the children's development? (See Chapter 4.)

Question 2 is 'Why should some children find it difficult to play?' The most obvious answer to this question would be that they did not have the opportunity, the maturation or the skills to do so. This, however, would engender important follow-on queries, e.g. 'When *should* children be able to play with others?' and 'What skills do they need and when should these develop?' It is also important to recognise that some children simply prefer not to play with others! After all, why should they? Preferring to play alone is quite different from being left out.

In this section, the children's difficulties in play are outlined. It has to be remembered that children with the same named condition can have different kinds of difficulties at different levels of severity. Also that boundaries between different conditions are often blurred and there is very often overlap, i.e. one child has elements of more than one learning difference, e.g. dyslexia and dyspraxia, or autism and Tourette's syndrome. This makes clear identification of difficulties problematic. Generally the most obvious difference is supported first, but staff must consider the other condition so that all difficulties are supported. What could these difficulties be?

Supporting difficulties

Sharing and taking turns

When at play, even very young children of 6 or 7 months constantly set themselves problem-solving challenges, e.g. 'How do I do this?, Where does that go?, If I drop my biscuit over the edge of my chair, does it disappear or is it still there?, What does this toy feel/taste like?, Do my toes look like my fingers?, How do they move?' This is sensori-motor play. At this stage children play alone and use all of their senses to focus on their own investigations for brief times, abandoning their research whenever something more interesting presents, but gradually they become aware of others playing nearby and move towards them. At this stage they are not really cooperating or sharing; they are playing alongside another child without evaluating what the other is doing. This is parallel play. But gradually children begin to play together and learn to share ideas and resources, and just as there are norms for all aspects of development, the times at when play scenarios should change are documented too.

These norms are helpful in delineating progress. They tell when changes should be happening (Table 2.3) and so help practitioners set realistic and appropriate expectations, but alongside knowing the different 'stages', these practitioners must take account of the children's temperament, e.g. are they outgoing and exuberant or anxious or reserved, preferring to wait and see? Also important are the previous play experiences the children have had. A child brought up with siblings has constant opportunities to learn to share and be involved in rough-and-tumble play while the single child most often plays alone. Perhaps this is why he enjoys being private? In the midst of all these differences, these norms do give guidance to the changing patterns of play behaviours even although health and safety concerns and the parents' work patterns mean that opportunities for outdoor play and even play with junk such as egg boxes and toilet roll tubes have been reduced!

These stages are the same for all children in all cultures. And as the play demands change, the social, intellectual, emotional and motor demands change too. Children with difficulties may not be able to make the transitions into more (intellectually, emotionally, socially and motor) demanding scenarios without support; and careful explanations of what is involved in the new way, e.g. allowing another child to share, may be required. Carol Gray (1996) advocates social stories to provide detailed understanding and overcome misapprehensions.

As play becomes more complex, as the children use resources and need a friend to play with, they are learning to share and cooperate and to take turns. When this happens naturally, when the children have their own reasons for so doing, sharing becomes part of the game. But when it is imposed from above, there can be less happy results.

Table 2.3 The changing patterns of play

Type of play	Age	Characteristics
Sensori-motor: early discovery about shape, texture, weight, taste, hardness, malleability	0–2 Solitary play	Exploration and perception Child discovering the properties of objects
Symbolic play: first signs of imagination/pretending	2–4 Parallel play, i.e. playing near another child without cooperating and with minimal interaction	Using one object to represent another, e.g. a yo-yo as a pet dog; a clothes peg as a doll
Simple construction: early recognition of patterns and tessellation	3+ Creating something with a friend: brief interactions soon abandoned. Children beginning to empathise with children with additional needs	Building towers (three blocks high) Enjoys stories, especially with repetition, e.g. the Little Red Hen
Pretend play: role play in context. Fantasy play becoming important	4+ Sustained play with a friend. Some small group interaction	Action songs enjoyed as balance and coordination improve Wider life experience allows taking roles of nurses, firemen, space games
Games with rules: football, chess, etc. Can make up rules for games	6+ Children begin to identify leaders and followers Play mainly in same-sex groups	Supporting teams; collecting team memorabilia

Source: Macintyre and McVitty (2003)

Many adults claim that 'learning to share and take turns' is a key part of nursery education and indeed it is, but from the child's point of view how frustrating it is to hear 'Why don't you share?' just when you have managed to get the lorry or the dressing up clothes to play the game that has been taking shape in your mind for ages. Why should you share? For sharing is more than the physical act; it involves explaining the planning and the ideas that are developing in your head. Listen to Sam:

> I'd been waiting to get the right stuff for ages and I had a good plan to build a spaceship with these boxes and things and then I was told to let Fraser play too. I shouted, 'No way' but he hung around and I got told to share. It was my idea and he wouldn't be any use at this game anyway. It's not fair! In my head, I was so angry that I wanted to push him away but that would get me into trouble, so I just went outside and sat under the tree. That was the end of my best plan.

Beset by good intentions to help 'left-out children,' practitioners need to take time to consider if intruding on play in this way *is* fair! Researcher David Cohen (1979) is one who thought not. He argued, 'When I hear that children at play, "*ought to take turns and share things*", I ask, *Are there social engineers on the swings?*' Even the mantra 'You can't say you can't play' has to be viewed with caution in my view, because there are times when children need to be able to resist sharing so that they can follow their own ideas through. Does anyone else agree?

Singly or together, at play the children need time to set challenges and find solutions. For often one problem leads to another, e.g. 'How can I make the margarine into a cake?' may become, 'If I make it too soft by beating it, how much flour will make it the right consistency to go into the baking tin?' And if the trials don't work, then it doesn't matter; the learning process based on the experience itself has been valuable and next time – or the next – the reflection that has come from the trial(s) should lead to a more successful outcome! And if it doesn't, well, there you are; in play children don't have to be 'successful' – if it doesn't work out, they can do something else. They don't need to have an end product at all. And, of course, in the process the intended cake can become something else entirely, for imagination knows no bounds.

So play can do all the following. It:

- can allow children to make choices and evaluate the success of their choice;
- can nurture children's learning as they experiment with things they like to do;
- can allow them to share if they wish or play alone;
- can let them abandon plans if they fall flat or if more exciting ideas come to mind;
- can give them time just to be or to make trials and errors;
- can let them visualise other ways, i.e. use their imaginations;
- can develop social, emotional, motor and intellectual skills;
- can let them act out worries and prevent them being sublimated.

And because what children often choose to do is a rehearsal for the everyday skills of daily living, then the practice can facilitate later learning, especially if the children can readily transfer what they have learned in one situation to another.

Using feedback and transferring learning

There are two vitally important concepts that should be part of observation and assessment. These are:

1   using feedback from one try to improve the next, and
2   transferring learning from one experience to another similar one.

How could practitioners know if children had been able to do these things? Example: picture a child running to jump over a rope supported on two skittles (Figure 2.8). If he is unsuccessful and his feet get tangled up in the rope, what does the child do next? Does he decide he must run faster, or alter the take-off point, or approach the rope more slowly to have time to judge the height? If he does any of these things – immediately or at a later try, he is remembering and using his first experience to ensure the next try is more successful. If this happens, he is using feedback successfully. And what about transfer? Well, observing his skill in perhaps jumping over a bench or jumping into the car efficiently could show that that skill had been transferred and formed the foundation of a more challenging action. Then, back at the setting or at

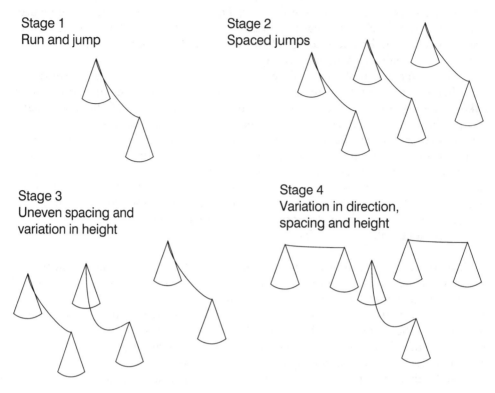

Stage 1
Run and jump

Stage 2
Spaced jumps

Stage 3
Uneven spacing and
variation in height

Stage 4
Variation in direction,
spacing and height

Figure 2.8 Stages in running and jumping

home, altering the layout of the skittles could add a spatial challenge. Observations like this could show if both feedback and transfer had been used to give a better result.

Imaginative play

Play activities are often used as evidence of children using their imaginations; however, these are not synonymous. Play can involve intelligent exploration, problem-solving, developing coordination and focus but not necessarily imagination. And of course imagination can be used in situations that are not playful. The core of imagination, whether playful or not, surely must be the capacity to appreciate what is not happening at this moment in time. Imagination has to work with knowledge and skills in order to produce something different, and that something may be useful or give pleasure or be mundane. Imagination is also the driving force behind creativity (Beetlestone 1998: 72). Some children will be naturally more imaginative than others; they can even terrify themselves by imagining 'ghosts and ghoulies' that become real. But sadly some have little imagination and are held in the here and now. Their play and their lives will be limited by this lack, and strategies to support this development have to be tried.

Interaction strategies

For young children, closed questions, e.g. 'What colour are your shoes?', are of limited value except to prompt recall, yet it is surprisingly difficult for staff to replace questions with statements that prompt longer or more imaginative replies. Some practitioners claim that statements are only pseudo-questions, but in questioning, the balance of power stays with the interrogator and the child is in a subservient role. Sharing ideas through using statements is a less threatening strategy, the notion being that the children will be able to imagine what went on and add linked ideas from their own experiences. This could be especially helpful for children with little imagination.

So, replacing the question 'What did you do on your holidays?' with 'When I was young, my family went to the beach and had a lovely time finding things on the sand and paddling in the rock pools' would hopefully prompt the child to share his own experiences and oust the usual reply, 'Nothing!' The fact that you had set the scene and outlined the expectation of a reply is much less threatening than a question that requires a correct answer or a boring one that needs no thought. And if/when responses to the statement do not immediately happen (for this new approach may take time, time for the children to relax and realise they can make a contribution), a more imaginative statement – 'I saw a little silver flying fish near the rocks one day' – might just encourage the child into the realms of fantasy.

Interaction practice: Think of a time when you want to interact with a reluctant-to-speak child or one who uses pedantic language. How could you encourage them? What experience could you share? Envisage the statements (often conceptualised by beginning with a question in your mind) and visualise three responses the child might make. Develop ideas as to how you would take each of these forward.

Another strategy is to encourage the child to play in a group with more imaginative children and give him time to ponder as you repeat the stimulating part of the other children's replies. Acting out very short stories that the children have made up is another ploy.

Listen to nursery nurse Amy explaining her success with Mark:

Mark (who was 5) was not interested in any of the creative work that I encouraged. He wanted to count bricks and had a fetish for tidying up, but he saw no purpose in the dressing up box or the firemen's hats or the large building bricks. And when his Mum came to collect him she would greet him by asking, 'Did you do your counting today?' so perhaps it wasn't surprising that he thought that the most important activity. When I tried sharing my experience, 'I used to pretend that one of my bricks turned into a friendly dog, because I'd always wanted a pet', he just gave me a pitying look as if to say, 'Well, that was mad.'

But then I involved him with a group of four other boys who could make up short stories, share them in a small group and then act them out. One of the teaching assistants scribed their stories and put then on the wall, and this proved a great incentive to make more stories. After some time on the perimeter of the group, Mark offered a story of his own. It was, 'It was windy but I ran onto the pitch and scored a goal.' And the children developed that idea into a football game. Mark was rather overwhelmed by his success but didn't have the confidence to be a player, so I suggested he became the 'ref' and he blew the whistle. The story was simple but it had the potential both for action, for reflecting on the feelings of the scorer and the goalie, and for discussions about different football teams.

I had never asked Mark to put forward a story but once he started he volunteered another one. He had thought it out and his Dad had written it out for him at home. The story was, 'When my bricks grow tall, we can climb up them to see the aeroplanes.' One of the group asked if they were magic bricks that could grow like Jack's beanstalk and Mark's eyes began to show interest in the different ways the story could develop. 'What would happen if the bricks grew when we were climbing up?' was Mark's most daring question, but when the others asked what was at the top of the tower and was it an airport control tower, then he saw that the other children were respecting his storytelling by listening carefully. Thereafter he became an integral part of the group and realised what fun it was to be imaginative.

What about children with learning differences; how can this apply to them? What conditions/syndromes have 'poor imaginations' as one of their indicators?

The actress and writer Jane Asher, who is a leading patron and fundraiser for the National Autistic Society, explains that children on the autistic spectrum 'lack imagination'. She tells that this lack is much more devastating than not being able to appreciate the subtleties or sequences within a story or having the capacity to imagine what it must feel like to be the little red hen or the rainbow fish or even to empathise with the lighthouse keeper who has found that the gulls have eaten his lunch, i.e. the usual manifestations of being imaginative. She explains, 'Without imagination, a child finds it impossible to remember the past, i.e. to remember yesterday and to visualise what tomorrow may bring.' For those who can do these things, it is almost impossible to imagine how limiting this must be.

The importance of routine

Understanding the effects of poor imagination, however, goes some way to explaining why many children on the autistic spectrum find comfort in routines such as punching the air or touching the doorpost six times before entering the room. Perhaps these actions help to fill the void created by not being able to imagine and they give the children security because they are in charge. For some time children on the spectrum can be bound by one routine; they won't allow their chosen routine to change. And then suddenly for no apparent reason it can be abandoned and another can take its place. This adherence to routine also helps to explain why children like a fixed and preferably visual timetable for their school day. If they know what's coming next, they can be ready, i.e. have the correct book and pencil, even if they cannot imagine the possibilities that the expected lesson will hold.

Many children on the autistic spectrum or who have dyspraxia or ADD/ADHD gain confidence through anticipating an unchanging routine. 'Surprises' that are intended to be treats, e.g. 'It's lovely day, let's go down to the park', just don't give pleasure, but instil trepidation and, in more extreme cases, fear of the unknown. Routine gives security. If it has to be changed, then teachers need to find time to explain why, and whenever possible give children advance warning of changes so that they can alter their plan.

Sharing

And when children at play are asked to share, to do this successfully they need to be able to visualise what is going on in the other child's mind. In so doing, they have to read non-verbal communication, another key difficulty for children on the autistic spectrum. This also applies when they have to follow the rules of someone else's game, for so many 'rules' are not written, they are developed as the play goes on; they are shared without words. But to be able to join in, children have to do two things. They have to be able to read the non-verbal signals of their peers and follow the sequence of events as they change. How complex it is for practitioners to try to provide explanations of what is going on for children who lack imagination.

Interestingly, games such as ludo or snakes and ladders or Monopoly can be understood, relished and played with skill because there is an intrinsic logic, e.g. If I land on a ladder I climb up but if it's a snake I slither down, while role-play scenarios or even stories can remain a mystery. Charlotte Moore has two sons, both with autism, and as she explains in her fascinating book *George and Sam*, the elder boy, George, loved hearing stories over and over again. She had thought he was deriving enjoyment from the storyline until, doubting this, she paused in reading the story of Little Red Riding Hood and asked, 'George, is the wolf good or bad, do you think?' 'Good,' replied George with no hesitation, 'because he is smiling.' So although George had enjoyed the rhythm of the words and the comfort of being read to, he did not have the imagination to understand the subtleties of the story or the fact that facial expressions can lie.

Imagination

Having too much imagination

But is it possible to be too imaginative? Can children be beset by so many possibilities that the only way to behave is to withdraw from the real ever-changing world and keep busy (because that is always approved) by twirling or flapping? One severely autistic child could only stand in a corner flapping one hand across his face. Was he cutting out events he couldn't understand and so reducing his distress? It took many months for his therapist to get him to enlarge the action so that a glimpse of the outside world was possible. While this was a lovely example of 'starting where the child is', the remoteness of the child meant it was almost impossible to assess any gain into his world.

Imagination and dyspraxia

Perhaps one of the lesser-known traits common in children with dyspraxia can be a vivid imagination. Miriam, Jenna's mum, explains:

Jenna has dyspraxia and the hardest part to cope with is her imagination. At this moment in time we can cope with her poor planning skills by organising her day round timetables and thinking ahead to foresee difficulties she might encounter; we can practise her movement patterns so that they improve, but the effect of being too imaginative is our worst fear. It really spells danger. She genuinely thinks she is a fairy and she wants to do everything that fairies do. She believes she *can* fly and if there's anything she can climb on, she'll jump off without realising she could break her legs. She would even jump out of windows to fly, because that's what fairies do. Although she's an intelligent child academically, she has absolutely no sense of danger. And then we worry about what she'll eat. Berries fascinate her, especially red ones, because she believes that these are the fairies' favourites. We keep waiting for her to be poisoned. Luckily, as yet there have been no ill effects beyond mild vomiting, but she has to be watched all the time.

However, she does tell fantastic stories. We often wonder where her ideas come from. Then the dyspraxia downturn means she finds difficulty getting her ideas written down on paper. But that's another story. Maybe she'll be an oral storyteller or writer of children's books – at least, that's what we tell her when her difficulties get her down.

Imagination: a future necessity?

Howard Gardner, the Harvard professor who in 1983, in his *Frames of Mind: The Theory of Multiple Intelligences*, alerted us to the 'eight forms of intelligence' and in so doing encouraged us to move beyond the 'three Rs' in assessing children, has focussed our attention again in his 2007 publication *Five Minds for the Future*. He berates Ofsted for having a narrow perspective in defining their model of competences and asserts that the skills and attributes needed for the twenty-first century are different. This is particularly relevant to this discussion on promoting imaginative thinking as a basis for creative thinking, which is really only possible once experience and maturation have brought expertise to bear. He defines the creative mind as 'one that breaks new ground – one that puts forth new ideas, poses unfamiliar questions and conjures up fresh ways of thinking' (cited in Stern 2007). In this description he is talking about mature adults in the workplace, but these skills cannot suddenly appear. As for any other competence, there will be a critical time for learning to be imaginative and if this is missed, it could be harder later on. For, as Gardner (2007) explains:

> Individuals develop very strong theories and concepts – often misconceptions – about the world when they are young. These ideas tend to become entrenched early on, and teachers regularly underestimate the strength and persistence of these formative ideas. Yet, unless these misconceptions are challenged, students are likely to remain with these early ideas or maintain them alongside the new and more adequate concepts. Thus, the dedicated teacher must find ways to undermine these early ideas and keep them from re-emerging.

When teaching children with learning differences, the emphasis is most often on helping them master the basic subjects or the coping skills of everyday living.

Can anyone really take enough time to find if they are imaginative or nurture an unusual train of thought? Do the imaginative children ever get enough credit for their imaginative outpourings if they can't write them down? If this is the case, surely the chance of missing potential stares us in the face? Can this go on?

Chapter 3

Early indicators of learning differences

Guess what,
Why is it that I take so long
To read and write and spell?
Why do others race ahead?
I ask, but no one tells!
Do people help? I hear you ask,
It's really hard to know,
'Keep trying' is the usual thing,
'Just keep up with the flow!'
I do try and try some more
Till I am sad and tired.
What's wrong with me?
Can it be
that I am 'wrongly wired'?
My head is clear; it makes a plan
So that should be OK,
But when the message travels down,
Somehow, it goes astray,
And leaves me with such messy work,
That I'm upset to see.
Each day I fail to make the grade,
I wish I wasn't me!

Christine Macintyre

When children come into Nursery or Primary 1/Foundation Stage, staff are often perplexed by finding that there is 'something' about the child that worries them, something they feel is not quite right, something that is causing the child difficulty. The child's parents may or may not be aware that something is amiss and of course, to complicate matters further, the difficulties may be context specific, i.e. they may not occur at home. Generally this eases concern, e.g. if the child speaks clearly at home but won't speak at school. This condition, possibly (s)elective mutism, would need a different strategy, i.e. to raise self-esteem and levels of confidence, rather than having a therapy to promote articulation or comprehension. Or the parents may suspect there is a problem but not know how to share their concerns, or with no other child to compare progress, they may hope they are mistaken and that difficulties will go away. Some will dispute that any difficulty is present and some will not appear to care. This is one reason why building positive relationships with parents is so important, for then concerns and strategies can be shared and form the basis of a positive, caring relationship.

The 'worries' that are listed in this chapter have been selected from the concerns of many early years staff. For each I have tried to provide insight into what could be wrong, why these difficulties might occur and what practitioners could usefully do to reduce their effects. But because there are co-occurring difficulties, there are also a number of general strategies and these can be effective for more than one group. Although children with different conditions have their own clutch of differences, no strategy suggested in the general group will harm any child, for they are the foundation of good teaching. In fact, it is best if these are practised with all the children because this prevents any notion that some are less able than others. The general strategies are followed by specific ones, e.g. finger/arm/shoulder strengthening activities for children with poor muscle tone, and later, in the appendices, there are introductory explanations of specific conditions to help practitioners understand more about what is wrong, especially if the children's difficulties persist.

General strategies

- Give the children more time to play, i.e. to make choices to experiment and to work at their own pace. For the older children, call it 'Golden time', but let the same play principles apply. Observe the focus and interest and very good behaviour that almost always results.
- Be positive. 'Catching them being good' and knowing the kind of rewards or praise the children prefer is the best way, but remember it can still be very difficult for children to comply in order to earn a reward. And even if the children appear impervious to praise at the time, they may reflect later and try to alter their behaviour on subsequent occasions. Then everyone will benefit.
- Focus on the things the children do well while paying attention to the competences that require support. Avoid *always* interpreting 'support' as dealing with difficulties, for boosting the children's confidence stimulates their motivation to keep trying. This is the best way to enhance the self-esteem.
- Keep the same routine or explain changes in advance whenever possible. Use a homemade picture timetable or a professionally produced one such as Boardmaker to ease anticipation of what comes next. This can help the children plan their day and gain a measure of independence.
- If speech is absent or difficult, use PECS (picture exchange system) or signing to facilitate independence and encourage single words. If this different method of communication arouses interest in others, all the children together might enjoy learning to sign as a shared (secret language) form of communication. (This needs to be checked with regional policies. Not all agree with using these methods because they consider that depending on an alternative method of interacting could delay speech.)
- Be careful where the children sit in class. For individual work, a quiet spot with easily distracted children facing into triangular panels can help them concentrate. Sitting a child who would benefit from calm near a child who provides a good role model can also be helpful. Sometimes sitting children at the back of the class can

be a good idea because then they feel their backs are protected and won't receive sudden, undesired signals such as brushing past or prodding. But if distractibility or hearing difficulties are present, the child must be near the teacher.

- Try to ignore minor upsets so that the child's name is not always being called out. Remember that what you see as encouragement, the child may see as harassment.
- Keep tasks short, except if the child is bright and thrives on complexity. Then short tasks can cause frustration. Gifted children can have learning differences and be frustrated by a lack of challenge. In an ideal world, 'the lesson should finish when the task is done' (Moore 2004).
- For children who can't focus, however, try to explain the length of the task so that the children can visualise 'getting done'. A large egg timer (often obtainable from the nursery) can give a visual indication of how much time a task will take or how much time is left to complete it, as 'You have 5 minutes left' can be meaningless to many children.
- Support children with planning and organisational cues, e.g. ask, 'What shall we do first and what resources will we need?' Complete one stage at a time. This minimises the stress of having to remember.
- Provide immediate feedback whenever possible and always begin with a positive statement. Vary the types of activities so that boredom doesn't set in. Give rewards readily to boost confidence, first of all ensuring that these are what the children wish to have!
- Allow chill-out time. Very often children can feel pressures building up, and knowing that they are allowed to be private for a spell releases the stress and helps them regain control and calm. Alternatively they may need to run around to let off excess energy in a safe environment. If they have Tourette's syndrome they may need to blurt out sounds or express their tics for a while. Knowing this can be done in private can reduce the urge to move or call out.
- Allow the children to use headphones that provide soothing music or white noise (seek advice from an audiologist). This can often bring their hearing to normal level and let them tolerate 'normal' classroom sounds. Or, as a first step, play soft, calming background music as the children play.
- Children may have little appreciation of cause and effect, so 'future rewards' as bribes to behave have little effect. Many are slower to learn skills such as self-management/problem-solving/coping with change. Avoid fluster by always allowing them extra time, e.g. at break to go to the toilet and at home time to gather their belongings together.
- If children find sitting still very difficult, allow them to sit on a beanbag – this allows a little movement. Also, provide a squeeze ball or clay to allow hands to work while the child is listening. These strategies can aid stillness and concentration.
- Have a daily timetable on view with the breaks clearly marked. Having a moving pointer attached to the timetable can help children recognise 'how much longer' the day has to run. However, this is quite complex, so explanations are required, e.g. 'Look, only this short time till Mummy comes, let's have fun.'
- Try to give some advance warning of changes in routine or of teaching personnel.
- Above all, teachers have to build a positive relationship with the parents and when necessary they have to explain that they appreciate the child's condition is no one's

fault. The parents may well be exhausted and over-sensitive to any seeming criticism. It is also less confusing if the children have the same set of rules at home and at school and if they appreciate that home and school are working together to support them.

- Trying relaxation exercises can help if they are done in an atmosphere of calm. These help body awareness and concentrating. Letting the strength flow out of the body into the air through flopping down or blowing out can help children to recognise tension in their bodies and show them a way to dissipate it.
- Watch carefully for any repeated stress play, e.g. smacking a doll with relish, as this just *might* be an outlet for abuse seen or suffered at home, but avoid jumping to conclusions. Keep a time/date diary and share observations with other professionals.
- Allow time for computer-based learning.

Computer-based learning

Many children cope better when they can use a computer. There are a number of reasons for this:

- The children can learn at their own time and pace.
- They do not have to read non-verbal communication that can be confusing.
- The computer gives immediate feedback and offers spell checks.
- Children can use each hand without crossing the midline.
- It is a socially approved strategy – it is 'cool'.
- It is reasonably private so other children don't check the level of work.
- The computer is 'anonymous' – it doesn't give out blame or disapproval.
- One child, when asked, 'Why do you like the computer so much?' replied, '*The computer doesn't have moods!*'

And, of course, the computer can produce enhanced work that motivates further endeavour. Then the children are encouraged by having something lovely to take home or show their peers. Furthermore, the fear of isolated learning can easily be overcome by having a time limit per session and alternating each session with times for free or structured play. Balance is the key to success.

Structured play

In structured play, the resources are set out so that certain skills can be taught, e.g. in baking, how to measure and weigh, or in craft work, how to carry scissors safely. The skills of daily living, e.g. preparing a meal, setting a table, getting dressed, tidying up, erecting a tent and endless others, can be demonstrated to show the most efficient way. In no way will this detract from free play. In fact, it will enhance it because of the wider skill base the children achieve. Ideally the skills will link to what the children have chosen to do so that they recognise the purpose and understand why certain ways keep them safe.

Gathering video evidence as a means of confirming observations and/or to procure specialist support

When the general strategies suggested in the list have not proved adequate in reducing the children's difficulties, it is a good idea to gather evidence of these on video. This allows practitioners to share their concerns with colleagues and watch the recording over and over again. If physiotherapy help is required, the clip gives an accurate dated portrayal, i.e. 'evidence' rather than an anecdotal story, and so can be an accurate form of communication. The recording can also be compared with others taken at a later date and so provide evidence of progress or indeed regression. It is a good idea to ask all parents for permission to film their children at the start of the year. The parents may also need to be reassured that the film will only be used for educational discussions among a select group of professionals who work with the children.

Parental permission is also necessary if specific programmes are to be used or if other experts, e.g. speech or occupational therapists, are to be consulted. Maturation and appropriate intervention can make a huge difference to children's competence, but, that said, no one should delay contacting experts in the field. It's always best to err on the safe side and cancel later if appointments are no longer required.

If practitioners suspect a specific condition is present, this observation should be shared with the line manager. Tests must be carried out by a psychologist, who will give the final diagnosis. Confidentiality is essential, as a basis for trust and positive relationships, so initial concerns should always be shared in private, not even in an open staff room.

Before 6 years of age, children are not likely to be given 'labels', and before considering/requesting a formal diagnosis it would be vital to ascertain both the pervasiveness and the level of each child's profile of difficulties. For practitioners who feel ambivalent about what to do, or if they are reluctant to be the one to make the difficult decision to inform parents about concerns, a useful yardstick is to ask, 'Does this difficulty *significantly* hinder the child?' Admittedly the word 'significantly' is subjective, depending on the perception of the practitioner, but attempting to answer this question can often help decision-making regarding procedures and taking steps to contact specialists. The second query should ask, 'If I change my input, to what extent will this alleviate the children's difficulties?' and if this raises possibilities, then these can be tried and evaluated before further steps are taken.

The areas set out in Table 3.1 provide a sample checklist that could be used independently by different colleagues observing the same child. Assessments made independently then compared would make the evidence more objective. In this checklist the categories are grouped, showing concerns that often occur together, but different children may exhibit just one in any box. As one teacher explained, 'It's reasonably straightforward if the children have evident difficulties in just one area but they often have snippets from several . . . do we try to add them up?' This comment led to the scoring scale 1–10 against each descriptor on the checklist, with advice to keep the scores separate. This is to enable assessors to discuss the content, to see the changing scores over time and gradually to draw up a more specific checklist that is appropriate for each child. This would lead to the compiling of more detailed observations in the categories that were awarded low scores (a score of 1 indicates low concern; a score of 10 indicates high concern).

The descriptors recorded on Table 3.1 are of different children. It is a cumulative chart. The observations are put together to show common observations. Each child will have a specific chart to show particular traits. After Table 3.1, the differences/difficulties are explained in detail.

It can be very difficult to assess whether these traits are transient, possibly in reaction to a new experience or whether they indicate an enduring condition. So one of the key

Table 3.1 A checklist to identify first concerns

Area of concern	Descriptions	Initials of staff: Child's score	Date and comments Plan of action
Hypotonia – (low muscle tone)	Is floppy; lacks strength. Finds everyday tasks difficult, e.g. zipping coat, placing things without them crashing down, using a knife and fork. Usually last to do things		20:5:09. Needs strengthening programme for fingers and hands Use clay, clothes pegs and jingles Contact physiotherapist; begin advised strengthening activities
Hypertonic: too much muscular contraction	Muscles appear stiff, restricting mobility. Tension in shoulders Appears fearful of new activity Reluctant to play outside		Relaxation exercises; play in warm water Play soothing sounds tape Check possibility of swimming in warm pool Massage
Can't crawl using the cross-lateral (C/L) pattern	Has difficulty with activities where crossing the midline of the body is necessary. When painting a rainbow, changes hands at the top of the arc to complete the pattern. Can't use a knife and fork		Use Tap Time* ensuring crossing the midline to tap knees, shoulders, heels on opposite side Check balance in crawling position. Try crawling up stairs (easier to feel and observe the C/L pattern)
Sensory hypersensitivity	Rubs eyes and is distressed by noises and lights. Won't touch clay or taste fruit such as kiwi fruit		Reduce environmental lights, colours, noises; try earphones? Use Theraputty**
Very restless; squirms in seat; always on the go	Won't stay still; can't concentrate; never finishes anything; shouts out; makes strange noises		Give choices and only short tasks. Try to ignore noises and shouts. Praise for any stillness
Listening and speaking	Can't listen; in a world of his own; no focus Can't speak: (s)elective mutism Speaks but can't be understood Pedantic speech Disappearing speech		Try repeating soft sounds; use toys that squeak or music boxes Use PECS Contact speech therapist Query autistic spectrum for disappearing speech
Comprehension	Doesn't understand instructions/ can't play with others		Simplify everything and ensure hearing/seeing is OK

Table 3.1 continued

Area of concern	Descriptions	Initials of staff: Child's score	Date and comments Plan of action
	Speech is clear but out of context		
	Query hyperlexia; in extreme cases, query Williams syndrome		
Poor planning and organisation	Never ready in time; puts clothes on slowly and in the wrong order		Use visual timetables for everything Allow extra time for understanding the order of events
	Can't anticipate events		
Memory	Can't remember what was learned yesterday		Give simple one-at-a-time instructions; break tasks down in stages – but pull together again to show completed product if appropriate
Reliance on routine	Strict adherence to routine; upset by changes		
	Obsessive behaviour		
Rhythmic difficulties	Can't beat out a simple rhythm or copy one		Play a 'question and answer' game with percussion
	Won't listen to nursery rhymes		Have stories that have repetition, e.g. 'The Little Red Hen'
Lacks empathy	Bullies other children and staff		Explain; work on feelings; use puppets to describe hurt
			If causing danger, restrain the child

Notes: *'Tap Time' is a jingle to teach body awareness and crossing the midline. Find it in Appendix 7.
** Theraputty is a type of clay used by occupational therapists. It does not leave traces and can be tolerated by hypersensitive children. Google 'Theraputty' for details.

assessments, apart from the severity of the indicators, is whether or not they 'last'. This is why dating assessments is so important and why regular checks over a few weeks should be made.

Specific strategies

The chapter will now develop the concerns that have been identified by practitioners, give explanations and offer play strategies to support the children's development. (Chapter 4 continues the idea of adapting play scenarios to match the difficulties displayed by children in meeting the demands of the activities of daily living and learning.)

1 The child is floppy; has low muscle tone; is last to do things

One of the common difficulties across different syndromes and conditions is hypotonia or poor muscle tone. Very often parents say, 'I knew from the start there was something wrong, my baby was so floppy.' Children with Down's syndrome, with dyspraxia, with dyslexia and of course cerebral palsy all have movement difficulties because poor muscle tone, not supporting the joints by holding them firm, hinders coordination and makes children clumsy. Also, the children may be slower to respond because they have to 'gear up' or take their movement plan to a conscious level before they can act. Children with enough muscular strength can do things spontaneously, and often with little apparent effort, but poor muscle tone causes delay and inefficient, often off-balance and certainly uncoordinated movement.

Listen to Ellie describing Daisy, who is nearly 5:

> Daisy is a happy child who means to cooperate, I'm sure, but the first thing we noticed was that she was always last to come to sit down, last to go outside to play and certainly last to get her coat on. It was such a struggle and we wondered why. The other children noticed and were getting irritated, especially if she made their group last to finish at tidy up time. 'Why do we always have to wait for her?' one impatient child blurted out, and at this point the staff decided Daisy had a real problem; she wasn't just reluctant to join in; for some reason, she was slow to get off the mark. When we wondered, was this a case of 'won't do' or 'can't do', we thought it was the latter. But what could be wrong?
>
> Closer observations showed that her movements lacked strength and because of this, fluidity. When she picked up a paint pot from the table, she used two hands and clutched it against her apron and then she had great difficulty releasing the pot into the sink without spilling the dirty water down her front. Watching her was like a slow action replay compared to the other children. When she caught a large ball, again she used the whole length of both arms to hold it secure, then she was very flustered trying to reposition the ball so that she could throw it. The throw was more of a whole body jerking action – we felt that the strength needed had to travel up from her stronger legs because her arms weren't able to throw on their own. So actually another child's hurtful remark had alerted us to a problem that we might have missed!

The following observations from different members of staff were discussed: (a) to consolidate 'impressions' and justify the preparation of a specific programme for Daisy; and (b) to give the staff confidence in sharing their concerns with Daisy's family.

When she holds her paintbrush, she holds it very near the tip and she holds her arm into her side as if it needed extra support. She stabs the paper rather than stroking it.

When she does attempt to climb on the frame, she stays near the foot; her hands give her some support but she doesn't often pull up; when she does try to climb, her shoulders seem to overextend.

She knocks into things. She doesn't make accurate spatial judgements so she spills water, and if there is anything heavy, she can't control it, so it clatters down.

> She has difficulty picking up small items for a collage and she covers them with glue, making a mess. Then she is upset.
>
> Before she moves, it's as if she has to gather her thoughts and decide what to do rather than just moving.

From a plethora of observations like these, the staff decided that they could justify their concerns and share their concerns with Daisy's parents. Although she could stand well and didn't really look any different to the other children, Daisy had poor muscle tone in the top half of her body, especially around her shoulders. She had reasonably strong legs and could run well but in sitting she slumped into herself or over her table. Her parents had noticed that she was 'a bit clumsy' but thought all young children tended to be so, especially if they were left-handed like Daisy. They hoped she would grow out of 'falling over thin air' (to quote her dad). Her mum explained, 'It is very difficult to show her how to do things because her left-handedness means that everything is the wrong way round!' While they were anxious that Daisy's problems had been significant enough to cause concern at school, they were pleased that she was to be given 'unobtrusive help' in terms of specific support within a group movement programme and later physiotherapy if that was still required.

Asked what they did in this 'unobtrusive programme', Ellie explained:

> We planned a programme that had finger, hand and shoulder awareness and strengthening ideas and this was carried out for all the children, with special observations for Daisy so that any improvement could be monitored. We tried to ensure that there was resistance, i.e. the upper body had to work hard to make sure there was the potential to increase myelin (i.e. the coating that surrounds the axons in the brain and strengthens the impulses that travel from one neuron to the next) and strengthen her fingers and hands. We concentrated on the *process* of doing things such as rolling firm clay rather than making objects.

So what were the key competences they were developing? These were strength, body awareness and timing of actions, remembering that while increased size of actions would help mobility, some resistance was needed to increase strength. Another key aim was to develop Daisy's ability to crawl using the cross-lateral pattern (see Table 3.2).

2 Can't crawl: the importance of using the cross-lateral pattern

Many parents whose children didn't crawl, i.e. who bum-shuffled, or crawled using a homolateral, i.e. a one-sided, pattern, or who went straight from sitting to walking without attempting the intervening skill, do not realise that this omission *might* cause problems, particularly with writing. This is because some children who didn't crawl couldn't crawl and so they missed the early stretching and reaching, i.e. spatial

Table 3.2 Some ideas to strengthen the top half of the body

Programme of activities	Observations: Teaching points
Baking. Mixing firm margarine in a bowl. Use the wooden spoon to chop the margarine before beating it. Use a second spoon to clear the margarine from the first	Allow the children to hold the bowl against their aprons. Encourage creaming the margarine. This means the children work at the midline of the body with two hands doing different things
Rolling clay (as firm as the children can manage) to make thin sausages and then wind them into coils	Observe the level of pressure the children can use. Make sure the hands are under the shoulders rather than out in front as the children roll the clay
	Coiling the 'worm' involves a good deal of squeezing the clay so this helps strengthen fingers and hands and the development of the pincer grip
Incy Wincy Spider and other rhymes	Children make their fingers into spiders and make them climb up the drainpipe
'Show me a strong spider' – hold it still; make its legs wobble, hold it still. Stretch it out to make a huge spider, and then crumple it up to hide when a seagull flies past	As the spider climbs, the children should adjust their balance to allow them to stretch higher
	Holding a strong spider shape needs strength and develops finger awareness – try it and see!
Use clothes pegs to make wooden deckchairs and other patterns or use them to hang up dolls' clothes	Ensure the children are sitting in a well-balanced position with feet well supported, as swinging legs inhibit balance. This also helps prevent them clutching the pegs to their fronts
This develops the pincer grip	
In the construction area, any kind of carrying and placing bricks strengthens arms and shoulders. Any supervised pulling and pushing activity is good too	Use skittles to form an obstacle course so that the children spend longer holding the heavy bricks as they take them from one place to another
Crawling through a barrel or sliding on the front, pulling along a bench	Observe how the children emerge from the barrel. (One child used his head as a lever because his arm strength was not sufficient to pull him out; see Figure 3.1)

awareness practices while in a safe, balanced position. Crawling also sets up a template in the brain that eases later learning, and so checking that all children can crawl, even if they choose not to do so, is vitally important.

Those who couldn't crawl might have difficulties with actions that involve crossing the midline of the body. Some children appear to have a 'wall' there and crossing over causes real problems. These can manifest in writing difficulties as well as a myriad of other problems, e.g. fastening zips, using a knife and fork, tracking words on a page, even painting a rainbow! Practitioners should look out for children who change pencils and paintbrushes from one hand to the other and check if they can crawl. Crawling up stairs and climbing on the frame use the same action, so activities can be varied while developing the same competences and having the same beneficial effect.

Think of the planning and sequencing involved in crawling. Which hand comes before which leg and what does the child do next? Try it and see!

3 Won't stay or join in. Can't settle. Restless. Separation anxiety

The first thing is to consider the age of the child, the previous experience in being separated from Mum and the child's acceptance of assurances that 'she will come back in a little while'. If these have been understood but haven't eased the distress, then the next step is to consider the environment. Is it too busy for a hypersensitive child? Are the walls too busy, the colours too brash, the sounds too loud and/or the lights too bright?

If the answer is 'no', the next questions to ask are, 'Is the child stressed?' or 'Does the child appear obsessed by moving around and, if/when aggressive, is he very difficult to restrain?, Is the urge to move overriding any entreaty/reward that is offered to stay still or calm down?' The differences between a child who is upset and irritable or one who has an extrovert temperament and the much stronger will of a child with an attention disorder is not difficult to spot – especially if the hyperactivity element is present. Children with the neurobiological difference ADHD feel their emotions so strongly that they feel overpowered by the urge to move. With ADD, the child may withdraw or stay on the sideline, preferring not to join in.

Urges and rewards

In some children, urges can be overwhelming. In adults, they are at the root of addictions such as gambling or alcoholism, providing evidence that out-of-control urges can destroy families and lives. In children, at a much-reduced level, these urges may be diagnosed as ADHD. They are often caused by a chemical imbalance in the neurotransmitters, e.g. the supply of dopamine in the brain. These urges can reduce when the frontal lobe of the brain, which gives control, is activated by maturation.

The main function of the brain is to keep the organism alive and reproducing (Carter 2004). To do this, it creates urges that strive to be satisfied. When we are hungry, our blood sugar falls and this urges us to eat. When we do so, 'feeling full' is the reward, and this satisfaction prevents us eating more. In extreme cases, just to illustrate the point, in Prader-Willi syndrome, the urge to eat is not followed by feelings of fulfilment and in the absence of reward the children eat more and gain enormous amounts of weight. Even though this makes them miserable, the children's urge to eat overpowers their rational thinking about the consequences. Their appetite is out of control. They have an addiction, so parents' begging them to stop eating just doesn't work. Even peer pressure and self-disgust are not enough to quell the urge.

Similarly, feelings of homesickness urge us to go home and the familiarity and the welcome there act as the reward; academic urges to succeed keep us studying; and altruistic urges to help others can lead to amazing selflessness and gains for charities. But taken too far, these might be regarded as obsessions.

There are many different kinds of urges stimulated by a feeling of emptiness that triggers action and this action should lead to the reward that gives satisfaction. Most of the time this cycle of stimulus, urge, action, reward is completed quite satisfactorily but sometimes it breaks down. In these cases either the urges fail to prompt the action (as in Parkinson's disease, when the ability to make voluntary movements is lost) or the reward from the action does not gratify the urge. Then the person feels bound to act again, straining after satisfaction. One notable professor suffered from Tourette's syndrome, which made him prey to bouts of being convulsed by tics (involuntary movements). Gradually over time he learned to control these so that he was able to lecture and participate in academic discussions. When he was asked why, when he *could* be still, he still had bouts of Tourette's, he explained that 'For a while I can concentrate and be still, but then I have to go into a private space and let the tics take over to get release from the tension that is building up inside me.' This explains the strength of the urge and the control required to inhibit it. No wonder many children can't make their bodies comply!

This kind of explanation would fit the case in children who were unable to be still. Despite knowing that they should be still, they are urged to move and move. Any other reward does not satisfy them and they appear out of control. In young children the reward centre in the frontal cortex of the brain is not yet fully activated. This explains why control can be achieved later, when maturation and myelination enable this area to function correctly.

So what can be done?

- Break the curriculum down into short tasks that have a chance of being finished and reward or comment on getting them done or keeping focussed even if the content is not correct.
- Let the child know you appreciate his difficulties and find a quiet private space where he can calm down.
- Assess the child's capacity to become involved in complex tasks – the complexity sometimes intrigues, so that the urges are quietened.
- Focus on the children's areas of interest whenever possible so that they have a chance to shine. Make sure the play resources suggest activities but recognise that activities may be rejected or abandoned.
- Try relaxation yoga-type exercises.
- Use lots of rhythmical jingles as they are short and enjoyable and they suggest an even, unhurried pace.

An interesting idea (Corlett 2006) is to ask practitioners to 'redefine the child', so that descriptors such as 'being out of the seat too much' are replaced by 'energetic and lively'. This group of psychologists call this 'reframing' (this is further considered in the notes on ADHD in Appendix 2).

Poor proprioceptive feedback

Another possibility is that the children's proprioceptors are not relaying information adequately. If this is the case, the children have to keep moving to energise them and so provide them with enough placement information to help them balance. If children are off-balance, they have to take steps to correct this before they can pay attention to anything else. There is a qualitative difference between this and the previous difficulty. These children can irritate their peers – and their teacher – by being restless or tipping over instead of sitting still, or nudging the child next door, but they don't have the tremendous urge to stand on their head or flail their legs or run hither and thither and appear totally out of control.

So what can be done?

- Allow the children to sit on a beanbag or a hedgehog seat (available from physio-therapists or occupational therapists). This often provides just enough movement to make the proprioceptors work.
- Encourage the children to play a piano and listen to the contrasting sounds that result from pressing on the keys firmly and lightly. This shows them that they can control the effects of their actions.
- Ask the children to write on a block of several pages with carbon paper between the lower sheets. They have to avoid marking the bottom sheet with the carbon.
- Have calming rhymes and jingles and encourage the children to repeat them slowly.

4 The importance of listening as the basis for speaking, reading, spelling and social communication

Listening is one of the key attributes of learning. It depends on sound auditory processing, yet children who have difficulties in this area are often described as uninterested or lazy, as if they had purposely chosen not to listen. And of course not listening or not hearing means that the children miss both teaching and the social communications from their peers. It is important to remember that many children, especially those with Down's syndrome, ADHD, dyslexia or dyspraxia, can have hearing difficulties that inhibit listening. For some time, it has been known that in Down's syndrome the children's smaller ear passages can become blocked by mucus and, as a result of not hearing the sounds of their own language at the correct time, some of the more severely affected children may never speak. Others will have a limited vocabulary.

A newer finding is that children with dyslexia may also have a hearing problem (Peer 2002). Neither group is deaf in the normal usage of the word, but both can be significantly hindered in speaking, reading and spelling, especially if the phonics method is exclusively used. And as 50 per cent of children with dyslexia also have dyspraxia, then many children with the label dyspraxia should be included in this hard-of-hearing group. Dyslexic difficulties of course can co-occur, or in the correct terminology be co-morbid with other conditions, so if the numbers of children who try to listen but don't really hear and so give up the attempt are added to those with recognised 'other' difficulties, the numbers of hearing-impaired children may be signifi-cantly higher than the statistics show. So poor listening is a developmental difficulty that is linked to a large number of conditions.

Often these difficulties remain hidden, yet testing whether children can differentiate between different sounds is easily done by going behind them, saying one sound quite quietly and immediately asking the children to say back the sound that they heard. Several trials of this informal 'test' can indicate whether professional intervention is called for. Perhaps, as many children use memorising or visualising to disguise their difficulty, all should be tested in this way?

One gem from Palmer and Bayley's (2004) *Foundations of Literacy* gives us pause for thought. A child asked by his teaching assistant why he didn't listen to the head teacher, replied, 'Well, you'll tell me again anyway!' Are we deafening our children by issuing too many requests to listen?

What is involved in auditory processing?

The first essential is accurate hearing. Children must be able to hear the sounds of letters clearly, relate each sound to the written symbol and store that learning in the auditory cortex so that recall can be fast and accurate when it is recreated vocally. Even at 1 year, children should respond to their name being called out even when the adult is behind them. (This is one of early tests for autistic spectrum disorders. If they do not respond to their name at 12 months, then their hearing/responsiveness must be checked.) Then the children need to blend one sound with the other letters that form a word. Increasingly, this has to be done quickly, for early hesitations inhibit the acquisition of reading and spelling skills. Poor hearing is a specific problem that does not signify low intelligence but if practitioners do not understand what is amiss, the two may be seen as synonymous.

What signs might suggest children might have listening/auditory processing problems?

- slow to respond to communications/requests;
- poor response to human speech but can hear environmental sounds;
- a history of ear infections;
- being better at maths than literacy topics;
- slow to speak and read;
- poor social skills/withdrawal from social occasions.

Sound therapy, e.g. the Tomatis programme, claims to stimulate the pathways that facilitate transmission between cells and the result is that the children become able to differentiate sounds more easily (www.tomatis-group.com).

So what can be done?

- Use only one signal, e.g. the jingle of a tambourine, to mean 'Stop, look and listen.' The continuous, soft sound means there is no jarring noise and the children have time to listen and respond.
- Practise this signal till every child has understood. At first, some children may need additional support, e.g. 'Are you ready to listen for the jingle?' before the sound is made.
- This idea can be developed in a game such as statues – the last child to stop and listen wears a red band but passes it on to the next 'late' child at the next turn. This prevents the idea of the late child sitting out when they are last and missing the very practice they require.
- Have a percussion treasure hunt. Hide percussion in the room and when the children find a piece they have to play it (Figure 3.1). All the children then describe the sound their piece makes and then name the piece that has been played. Some suggestions made by the children trying this were:

> Triangle: Tingle, ping, sing, jingle
> Cymbal and beater: Boing, boom
> Drum: Bang, boom, snap

Maracas: Serrch, scrunch, baroom
Indian bells: Ting, ping, bjonnnnng (making a drawn-out sound that stops when the bells cease).

- Once the children have found their percussion, the next task is to find how they can make the sounds last longer. The children have to listen to each piece and clap when the sound disappears. This develops listening skills and fine motor control as making the sound last requires gentle handling of the percussion.

Figure 3.1 The children are listening to percussion and accompanying it using voice sounds

Old favourites: tracking games

- Children stand in a circle with one child blindfolded, seated in the centre with a beanbag in front of his feet. The other children (the teacher points at one or two at a time) stalk in to try to retrieve the beanbag. If the child in the centre hears the approach, he calls out 'Stop' or 'Bang'. This encourages listening and careful stepping and is lots of fun. Any child who does not want to wear the blindfold can simply close his eyes.
- Another circle game that develops listening skills needs one large ball. The children stand in a circle and as the one in the centre with the ball makes a throw to a friend on the outside, he has to call out that child's name and tell him what to do. The action takes the child into the centre (carrying the ball) or, for more skilled movers, round the outside perimeter, then back to the centre and the game begins again. Examples might be: Harry – Hop, Rosie – Run, Louise – Leap, Danny – Dart, Billy – Bounce, Jack – Jump, Marie – March, Thomas – Twist, Sam – Stalk. Of course,

not all the children's names lend themselves to alliteration but when they do, it adds to the fun.

5 Speaking fluently and clearly

Babies are tuned in to learn to speak even before they are born. This can be seen – or perhaps felt would be the better word – when the babies' kicks in the womb cease so as to allow the child to listen to the mother's voice. And even at a very young age, babies will kick and turn their heads to the sounds of voices, especially to the mother's voice. From a few weeks old they will initiate 'conversations' by gurgling, thus keeping the adult entranced. Huttenlocher (1998) claims that the frequency of parents speaking to their children has major implications for their language development throughout their lives. He asserts that the more language children hear, the greater will be their vocabulary and this holds whether the children understand the words or not.

This has huge implications for children who are put in front of the television, because although words are heard, there is no two-way communication. Nor are the words modulated to the receptivity of the child as in 'motherspeak'. Unfortunately, mobile phones accompany some parents to nursery and talking to the child suffers.

'Proper' language starts in the second year when the two major speech areas that lie separately but side by side in the brain are activated. One is Broca's area and this deals with articulation, while the other, Wernicke's area, copes with comprehension of speech. It is important in any assessment of speaking that practitioners differentiate between the ability to articulate and so communicate effectively and the ability to understand. Many children who lack speech or show speech delay understand much more than they can say. Especially true in Down's syndrome, this differentiation is important in deciding both the level of speech in interactions and the amount of non-verbal support that is required. Table 3.3 shows the stages of checking, listening, speaking and comprehension.

In the earliest years, language develops in both hemispheres in the brain but by the age of 5, it shifts to the left side of the brain, often named the language side. At birth children are international, i.e. they are programmed to learn any language, but by 3 years of age, this faculty diminishes. Unfortunately, 'the plasticity of the brain's language circuits exists only during a limited time frame' (Winston 2004). This is why learning another language becomes more difficult with passing time. It shows how total immersion in the earliest years is the best way to be bilingual. Children who are totally deprived of opportunities to learn to talk may well have a physically different brain. They may use the right side to speak, not the much more usual left. Interestingly, about 5 per cent of people do this and usually they are left-handed (Carter 2004).

Left-handed children and language

Whereas more than 90 per cent of people are right-handed and have their language areas in the left side of their brains, the pattern is different for left-handers. About 5–8 per cent of children will be left-handed (anecdotal evidence says the numbers are increasing), but 70 per cent of that number still have the language centre in the left brain. The other, smaller number have their language areas in both sides (Carter 2004).

Table 3.3 Checking listening, speaking and comprehension

Age	Action		
5 YEARS	Can interact in groups; can focus amidst distractions Ready to sit for short spells and to wait for a turn	Can sequence a simple story without pictures; can anticipate endings and suggest appropriate alternatives	Articulates clearly and enjoys and composes simple rhymes, e.g. 'The fat cat' Can beat out a rhythm and repeat a heard one accurately – showing soft and loud tones
4 YEARS	Uses imagination to develop play ideas – fantasy play – will share plans/descriptions Girls especially will want to write their names	Can identify some colours. Has favourite stories and can find them in books. Enjoys repetition with no change	Uses complete sentences including pronouns. * Note use of/omission of personal pronouns Recognises that others have a different perspective, i.e. they 'see' different things
3 YEARS	Asks adults to share experiences, e.g. 'Look at the wiggly worm on the path' A small number will be able to read	Begins to understand directions, e.g. under, through, on top of Constant questions, e.g. 'Why . . . but why?'	Will recognise/copy/enjoy different emotions and facial expressions, e.g. grumpy granddad
2 YEARS	Can point out single objects and match them to pictures Begins to copy other children Shows frustration if thwarted; for some, time of the 'terrible twos'	Begins parallel play – more aware of other children and their movements/concerns. Asserts self through the use of 'No'	Holds eye contact longer. Uses three-word phrase;: 'sings' rhymes and songs, especially action songs
18 MONTHS	Uses objects appropriately; points accurately; begins to recognise turn taking through games such as peek-a-boo	Carries out simple tasks, e.g. bring teddy over; open your mouth wide; watch out of the window for Daddy's car	Can use 10 words; tries out new utterances; enjoys nonsense words. Will attempt to repeat baba or tttt, i.e. first phonics
1 YEAR	Monosyllabic babbling: enjoys making noises; recognises effect on others	Follows simple instructions e.g. come here, clap hands; wave goodbye. Holds eye contact and reacts appropriately to frowns and smiles	Turns head in response to name being called from behind.** (Very important to note this.)

Handedness is established before birth. Children even show a preference for sucking one thumb in the womb! (Google 'Anything Left-Handed' or go to www.ru-left handed.co.uk for equipment and advice on teaching left-handed children.)

Both Kuhl and Winston make important linked claims. They explain, 'We are all born with the innate competence to recognise the sounds of language as opposed to other sounds' (Kuhl 2000), *but* 'our brain depends on the right sort of environmental stimuli to get the process up and running' (Winston 2004). These claims lead us to understand that if children are overwhelmed by environmental stimuli, then this has a hugely negative effect on the acquisition of speech. So could the first step in reducing a language difficulty be to reduce the environmental stimuli that surround and possibly overwhelm the child?

Speech 'errors' in childhood

Around the age of 3 or 4, children become able to convey complex meanings through speech and as they do, they make 'errors' which could mistakenly be assessed as regression. Winston (2004) gives the example of children who used words such as 'ran' and 'held' correctly, but apparently regressed, falling back on 'ed' additions, e.g. I ran-ed and I held-ed. But this is really progress, for while the first attempts were imitations of speech they had heard from their parents, the second were evidence of the children recognising and attempting to apply complex grammatical rules. This only comes into play when the child has a sufficiently large vocabulary to need such rules (ibid.) and generally they pass through this stage without intervention.

But of course there are many difficulties that impede this progression.

1   Poor muscle tone in the lips, soft palate and tongue can prevent clear articulation even when the children understand what they want to say. Speech therapy is essential to help children make themselves understood (see Figure 3.2). The earlier this happens, the better, as children's confidence and self-esteem will suffer when no one understands what they say.
2   A psychological speech difficulty: (s)elective mutism. It seems strange that children who can speak clearly and readily at home can be affected by a condition that prevents them speaking – perhaps for years at a time – in any situation or environment where they feel stress. Some time ago this condition was called 'elective mutism', i.e. it was thought that the people affected were choosing not to speak, but newer research shows that their extreme anxiety forces them to remain silent. Despite desperately trying to speak, they just cannot make any sounds. One 8-year-old boy, apparently confident and certainly a high achiever at school and on the sports field, in the security of his home explained, 'I try and try to force words out. I know what I want to say and I know that not speaking is really holding me back, but my throat freezes and a huge block of ice prevents any sound escaping.' Another boy who was an excellent footballer was made captain of his school team. The staff hoped that total involvement in an atmosphere where children were making a noise might reduce his need to be precise and not get things wrong. But for many months the team was guided by gestures, not words. After a considerable time, one word did escape and slowly his vocabulary grew.

Figure 3.2 A speech therapy game. In this game the children learn to say separate sounds and practise them till they are clear. This should be kept as fun, e.g. Thomas the tank says? Answer – t, t, t. Then the child can stand in the centre of a display of items (drawn by the children or cut from magazines) and jump onto the ones beginning with the chosen sound – saying the sound aloud as they do. Gradually different sounds are added and then blends, so reading and speaking go together as they should.

What can be done to help?

- Be positive and smiling to build the child's confidence.
- Interpret the child's gestures accurately – the teacher making mistakes in the hope that the child will give the correct answer does not work.
- Do not repeat what the child should have said or over-articulate, for this can be demeaning.
- Find opportunities for the child to shine.
- Above all, avoid forcing the children to respond. They will only be able to do this when they have overcome the psychological barrier that keeps them mute.
- Some children can participate in group activities but for others this makes things worse so one-to-one interaction is most comfortable and rewarding for them.

Children with this condition should be seen by a developmental paediatrician because without a correct diagnosis, the wrong one, possibly autism, may be given. In that case support would be inappropriate. Although children on the autistic spectrum may also be selectively mute, they display other behaviors – hand flapping, repetitive behaviors, social isolation even among family members (not always answering to their name, for example), sensory integration difficulties and poor eye contact. These are not evident in selective mutism.

Out-of-context speech

When this difficulty is present, children can speak fluently, even excessively, without their words making sense to the recipient. Articulation can be splendid but when words are taken out of context they lack meaning. Often this different use of language suggests autistic spectrum disorders, perhaps Asperger's syndrome. Naturally children are upset when their friendly overtures are rebuffed. Sometimes the children's parents will try to give them ideas, e.g. 'Tell your friends you went to Spain for your holidays', but the child, possibly after practising to get the phrase word-perfect, finds a group talking about something completely different, bursts into the conversation and is met by silence or incredulity or, worse, hostility, as his word-perfect but out-of-context contribution sounds so strange.

Possibly to prevent recognising rejection, some children will keep talking at great length while their listeners flag and look for ways to escape. The dinner party bore is a mild example. At the extreme end of this continuum, there is a condition called Williams syndrome.

Williams syndrome

In Williams syndrome, 'the linguistic vehicle is grander than the messages it has to convey' (Carter 2004). Children who have this condition will appear as fluent talkers but the content of what they offer is vacuous. They often have a sound grasp of grammar and an extensive vocabulary but there is no depth of understanding in their conversations. In a busy setting it is not difficult to see how this syndrome could be missed. Affected children can appear very confident and outgoing, yet have great difficulty in following instructions and will be unable to complete a simple task, e.g. bringing two named objects from a selection of toys. The average IQ of children with Williams syndrome is around 65–70, much the same as for most children with Down's syndrome.

Assessment of speech

If 'length of utterance' was used as a criterion for success, children with Williams syndrome would gain a high score. Some can expound long lists of names of animals; even all the complicated dinosaur names can be spoken with ease. But of course quality, i.e. meaningful speech rather than quantity, i.e. rote-learned lists, is what is important. How much more difficult is it to assess that? Again, gathering evidence by tape recording is the best way because then the out-of-context nature of speech can be recorded and shared with a speech and language therapist.

What if speech disappears?

One of the most worrying things for parents is when their child who had begun to speak, regresses and becomes silent. Children who are later diagnosed as being autistic can show this trait. However, there are other reasons. When children are stressed, they often regress to an earlier stage of development. This tends to be a temporary state and once they relax and gain confidence their speech returns and they quickly catch up with their peers. Children on the autistic spectrum would have additional signs such as hand flapping, poor eye contact or missing responses.

For information on stuttering and cluttering and other speech impediments, go to www.afasic.org.uk or www.afasicscotland.org.uk.

6 Planning and organising difficulties

In the early years, it can be quite difficult to spot planning and organising difficulties because adults tend to do a great deal of this for the children – just to save time as much as anything else. Yet it is important to check whether children are able to plan and organise, as a difficulty here is common across many if not all conditions that house learning differences. At home, parents may have suspected that there was a problem if the children are never ready in time or if, beyond 3 years, they do strange things such as putting their clothes on in the wrong order, e.g. pants over trousers, or if they constantly forget instructions. The difficulty increases as independence is required, and being disorganised can really spoil lives. This can occur despite a high level of intelligence.

Laura, a final-year graduate, explains:

> People tell me I'm crazy to give up when I'm nearly a primary-school teacher but teaching means constant planning and organising and, even worse, coping when changes happen. Student life has only been manageable because good friends checked that I had the correct books for different topics and they made sure that I knew the way to different lectures and seminars. So I thought that with extra preparation I'd manage, as I've always wanted to teach young children. But final placement was a nightmare. Single lessons were fine, I could cope with that, but when several came together, I had to plan where all the resources were set out in the class and as the children all finished their work at different times and had to know what to do next, it was truly impossible. To make matters worse, I had a set of twins in the class and when I saw one, I wasn't sure which it was or what that one should be doing. That was the final straw. The class teacher saw I couldn't cope. I was devastated but I couldn't survive that much pressure. If teaching had been like the old days when all the children did the same thing at the same time, I could have managed, but not now, especially when some of the children wouldn't do what they were told the first time. That meant instructions for them had to be repeated and they played up. So I had to decide teaching wasn't for me. It was also so hard to explain to my family what was wrong.

And of course poor planning and organisation is a key part of dyspraxia, dyslexia, ADD and ADHD, yet these competences are often overlooked because of the immediacy in first dealing with the more obvious difficulties within each condition.

What could be the signs and symptoms of poor organisation and planning?

1   arriving late; getting lost; never able to find the way;
2   distressed by having the wrong books/equipment;
3   looking blank when told to get ready/get dressed/find a coat or a book;
4   watching other children to see what they are doing rather than starting off at once;
5   using delaying tactics to give more preparation/thinking time;
6   rushing work to prevent being last or late;
7   being silly to deflect attention from the real difficulty.

So how can we support children with this difficulty?

- Use visual timetables (pictures for the younger ones). Constantly refer to them so that children recognise their use. When they ask, 'What shall I do next?' refer them to the timetable rather than telling them what to do.
- Actually getting the children to draw their own timetables is a good idea as the activity reinforces the order of events.
- Make the timetable in the shape of a daily plan. Use small pictures in each box. If these are done on card or laminated at school then they can be physically changed with explanations as to why this was necessary. This saves last-minute crises. Once this has been achieved, build a two-day plan and eventually a weekly plan. This also serves to show the children how they have improved. The key is to simplify what has to be remembered so that the child retains a measure of control.
- After an explanation, ask the children, 'Now tell me what you are going to do' and then ask, 'I wonder what we will need to begin?
- Break activities down and complete one part before mentioning the second.
- Use picture sequences but explain why they have been produced, e.g. to help reflection and future planning.
- Stimulating recall to support planning difficulties like this can be time-consuming and frustrating if in the midst of the endeavour the child wants to go off on his own ploy, but with perseverance it's often possible to find that he can sequence events, and this is the basis of planning and organising. Then the secret is to help the child transfer that experience to other situations.

Discussion about the sequence of events to clarify planning and organisation.

T = teacher   K = Kieran, who has planning difficulties

T: (Showing photo sequence) I remember how everyone enjoyed playing in the leaf pit.
K: Aye, it was fun getting all covered up.
T: But we had to work hard before we played in the leaf pit, didn't we?
K: Uh huh.
T: Tell me what we did first of all.

SILENCE

T: Can you remember what we did when we went outside?

K: I got the big rake and me an' Gordon went round the back.

T: To find?

K: Lots of leaves and conkers and things and a dead mouse. We threwed him away.

T: And then?

K: Jumped in the pit and got covered up.

T: Was there anything in between?

K: Nup.

T: I wonder who were the boys who gathered most leaves?

K: It was me and him and we got big lots and piled them in and then we all jumped in!

T: So first, you gathered all the leaves, then piled them into the pit, then jumped in. Is that right?

K: Aye, three things to do 1, 2, 3.

T: Wonderful, you remembered how to make a plan!

Figure 3.3–3.5 Gathering leaves

Figure 3.3–3.5 continued

What other events lend themselves to emphasising planning in this way? A very useful sequencing practice comes in oral storytelling as the children can recap 'what comes first – and what comes next', e.g. 'When the three little pigs decided to leave home, what did they have to do first of all?' Or 'When Goldilocks went into the house of the three bears, what did she think about first of all?' or 'When Jack decided to plant the beans, I wonder what he'd need?' So checking planning skills actually adds focus and richness to the discussion as it stimulates different ideas about feelings or what might have happened. It is also important to note that although there are questions suggested here, they are open questions that do not depend on one correct answer, so they stimulate alternative solutions and shouldn't cut down any potential discussion.

Planning a picnic is another activity that lends itself to focussing on planning. The picnic can be for the children themselves or the toys in the room. They can discuss where to go (first decision), how they are to get there, what they will do, what they will have to eat, who is to carry the food, and so on, thus developing a linear sequence of events.

With children a little older, using SCOPE as a reminder of the planning process can help.

S: Search for ideas.
C: Consider one or two good ones.
O: Organise the resources you'll need to carry the plan through.
P: Plan the sequence, i.e. what you will do first, then next, then last.
E: Explain what you did, what bits went well and what you might change next time.

For children with planning and organising difficulties, practitioners should analyse activities in terms of the necessary planning and sequencing necessary to carry out tasks. Swimming is a wonderful activity for children who find these competences demanding, because the water aids their balance and allows them to focus on coordinating the strokes. But, in addition, if practitioners can explain what to do first and then next, e.g. 'Pull through the water with your hands and *then* kick' (or whatever the sequence of the particular stroke is), the planning part is emphasised. There is also the complex planning in getting changed into swimming gear and then dressed again. There are innumerable planning practices inherent in all activities if practitioners are given time to analyse the activity and gauge the type and amount of help that is required.

Planning can also be stressed when the children work outside on apparatus outside by simply asking the children, 'Tell me what you are going to do.' This slows down the impulsive ones and makes them think through the organisation of the activity. The extra time also helps children to balance well before going on the next phase of the movement (see Chapter 4).

7 Not remembering: poor recall, part of most learning differences

It can be very frustrating for parents, teachers and the children themselves when they know something one day and completely forget it the next. The teacher has high expectations and is met by blank looks! How much worse for the child to realise that things he should remember can't be retrieved. But why should this be? This is an important question because without good recall there is no solid foundation to support further learning.

Memories consist of many different things. Most children will be likely to remember their first school and be able to picture their first pet. Once they have learned to ride a bike, they will store that skill in their procedural memory and even if it is unused for some time, it can be recalled and used again. They will remember their family, hopefully with affection, and any emotional events such as going into hospital, and usually they will have a memory store of things they have enjoyed at school.

Each type of memory is stored and retrieved in a different way and many parts of the brain are involved. So it is not easy to give remedies for poor memories.

Various authors have suggested techniques, e.g. Mind Mapping (Tony Buzan's www.imindmap.com), where items to be remembered are conceived as a map with associated pictures. This is a pictorial form of timetabling, i.e. creating order from a plethora of disassociations. I would attest that the topic map used in teaching is a form of this as it links different subjects and makes them meaningful. Unfortunately in my view, the idea was taken to extremes, far beyond its remit, and then it was ridiculed. In my experience, it provided a sound way of making memories and plans visual and I hope in the cycle of educational events, it will re-emerge.

Empathy: understanding and supporting others

Although this aspect comes last in this chapter, it is very important. Particularly with children with learning differences, difficulties or disabilities, empathy received, empathy shared and, if necessary, empathy taught should be a prime concern of education. The policy of inclusion has made this even more critical if classrooms are to be free from children who bully. Sadly, being bullied seems to be the fate of many children with learning differences as well as others who are 'different' even in the most unobtrusive way, e.g. wearing spectacles or having red hair. Charlotte Moore, mother of two sons who are autistic, claims, 'Children who are different will be bullied, it's par for the course.' What a very sad reflection on our society! No wonder Howard Gardner (2007) has listed 'ethical' as a descriptor in his recent book, *Five Minds for the Future*. Those who bully must lack empathy. Unless they are sadistic, or have no experience of care in their own lives, surely they must recognise the effect their actions have on those that are less able to defend themselves?

So how does empathy develop and what can we do to promote it? Children are not born empathetic and the development of this trait in some ways mirrors the development of play. For in the first two years or so, the children are egocentric – the time when they engage in solitary play. But gradually the children are expected to become sociocentric, and episodes of turn taking and sharing and listening to stories about the resolution of dire deeds, e.g. the stepmother's cruelty to Cinderella, develop this.

But some children may be delayed in appreciating that others have feelings and goals different to their own. They may need longer to observe or explanations of things other children do intuitively. Some children will be so bound up in themselves that they need to be told that other children have worries and troubles and that they should be kind. Giving children appropriate responsibility is a key strategy even if the task needs to be spelled out more than once, because conveying high-as-possible expectations is a sure way to boost self-esteem. And once the children have self-knowledge and have gained self-worth, then they are ready to appreciate how others experience their world.

Chapter 4

Analysing and adapting play opportunities, particularly for children with learning differences (SEN)

When I go to school each day,
I know there's time to play,
There's lots of toys and girls and boys,
What shall I do today?
I'd like to play with the big red truck,
If there isn't too much noise,
But usually, with my bad luck,
It's surrounded by big boys.
I can't bear messy things like clay,
And dressing up's no good.
What does it mean to wear strange clothes?
I wish I understood!
The bricks are best; I line them up,
Red, then white, then blue.
I love the patterns that they make,
It's the best thing that I do.
I really enjoy the water tray,
I make things sink and float.
At the sand I build a castle
Surrounded by a moat.
There are so many things to do
And we get to choose,
And so we win and know that we
Need never, ever, lose!

Christine Macintyre

Analysing opportunities for play

In the photocopiable resources found in this chapter, activities have been subdivided into the four domains: intellectual, motor, social and emotional. This is done:

- to show the kind of learning that is possible in different learning areas;
- to provide a clear focus for observation;
- to show how considering the resources and making slight changes can optimise learning for all children and especially for those with learning differences (SEN);

- to provide evidence of the myriad of learning opportunities within play experiences.

Some people might suggest that dividing up learning in this way is slightly artificial as all four aspects continuously interact but I believe that this strategy helps focus observations. It also outlines the variety of opportunities within each area. This is even more important when children with learning differences are participating, for they may need extra support in making decisions and following their plans. The division can also suggest where interventions to support particular needs can be made.

In addition, the process of analysing the children's learning strengths and differences can readily be recorded through using this model simply by ticking the competences they have achieved and working on those that are in progress. And after the analysis comes the synthesis, i.e. pulling the strands together again to give a holistic picture or an overview of development. One example of this could be children mastering throwing and catching a ball. While this is primarily a motor skill, the children have also learned about distance, direction and rhythm, i.e. they have made intellectual gains. And then they can play competently with a friend; perhaps they might even join in a team game and this enhances their social, intellectual and their emotional development. Such achievements give their self-esteem a huge boost, especially if they link their achievements to watching and talking about local clubs or high-level sport. But to achieve this kind of success, analysis should precede synthesis, because this is the way specific profiles can be accurately compiled, appropriate interventions designed and gains recorded.

Expectations should be high but also realistic. Children with learning differences will have difficulties achieving some of the usual goals of development, and teaching strategies have to consider appropriate amendments. For example, children on the autistic spectrum will have key difficulties in the social aspect of their development so support in that area needs to be given priority, while not neglecting the others. Children with dyspraxia, on the other hand, will primarily have movement learning difficulties so the emphasis for them would be on the planning and the demonstration of motor skills. Children later found to have dyslexia may first show early difficulties with rhythm and so a focus on using percussion or rhythmic jingles would benefit them most. And of course the children with the attention deficit disorders, unless they are gifted and thrive on complexity, need short intellectual inputs with breaks to allow them to dissipate energy and settle, ready to pay attention. Children with Down's syndrome need particular support in the intellectual and motor areas, so making input visual and checking resources for size and flexibility to ease gripping can help them develop the key skills of everyday living. The emotional strand is important for every child as increasing confidence is a key priority in enhancing self-esteem. And within that, the development of empathy and altruism, the basis of a theory of mind, needs to be observed and if this does not develop naturally, explanations and opportunities for demonstrations of looking out for others and appreciating that they may have a different perspective to one's own have to be provided.

So this method helps observers tease out the complex list of competences and gives observation a structure. It ensures that intervention focuses on the areas that needs most support and gives practitioners confidence, both in justifying what they do and in showing the children's progress.

Table 4.1 Some difficulties that cross 'labels' and make playing hard work

Intellectual difficulties	*Movement difficulties*
• Not knowing what to do • Not being able to follow the unwritten rules of someone's game, so not contributing appropriate ideas to take the play forward • Having a poor memory, so forgetting yesterday's play ideas • Having too many ideas but not being able to plan or organise play resources or ideas • Not understanding/being able to cope with changes in routine	• Not being able to balance on stepping stones or on a bike • Being clumsy and knocking into others • Being too active and out of control • Being uncoordinated, especially at the midline of the body, so spilling water, messing up puzzles • Inability to grasp/release items • Unable to throw or catch a ball • Body build difficulties, making children avoid movement practices
Social difficulties	*Emotional difficulties*
• Being unable to communicate effectively • Poor articulation, making interaction difficult • Being too timid to join in • Being reluctant to share or wait for a turn • Snatching rather than asking • Preferring to be alone – all the time • Only wanting what someone else has	• Being unable to understand pretending • Lack of imagination to develop play ideas • Poor concentration; little focus or staying power • Inability to understand what someone else is thinking or feeling, so responding inappropriately • Not responding at all • Completely immersed in own solitary play • Aggressive when thwarted • Poor empathy and altruism, so unable to understand other children's perspectives

In the following pages, analysis is followed by possible amendments based on the difficulties each learning difference/SEN condition holds. It is important to remember, however, that because there is not a 'typical' child for any learning difference or special needs condition, the activities suggested may need further amendment to suit particular children. Table 4.1 presents some difficulties that can occur with different difficulties and make playing hard work.

The aim is that the children learn in a meaningful context. The key is learning to play. If skills are taught, they should be part of the play rather than being taught in isolation. Adding things like words on cards can be incidental additions: 'Oh, look, this card says "cake". Can you put it beside a piece of cake?' This can be helpful if the children are interested in learning words but should not spoil the flow of the play.

Scenario 1 Setting the table: having a tea party

Aim: Supporting children with learning differences (SEN) in the house corner

Most children with Down's syndrome are socially able and enjoy role-play. They will happily take the part of different family members and will interact with other children with confidence even if this is mainly through non-verbal communication. So in the

Intellectual

Role play — Mother, father, baby, visitor, pet dog

Choosing healthy foods for tea — Fruit, seeds, nuts, sandwich fillings, pitta/brown bread

Discussing what to buy — Menus for lunch — where to buy vegetables/flour etc.

One-to-one correspondence — Spoonfuls at baking time

Counting — Setting the table, matching, sorting

Imagining — What different visitors, e.g. aliens, would like to eat

Movement (motor)

Dressing and undressing — Doll/baby hanging up aprons, coats

Preparing food — Baking, chopping, washing, mixing, shredding, spreading, arranging on plates

'Ironing' — Flattening and folding tea cloths

'Writing' — Picture 'invitations' to the tea party

Learning in the house corner

Sharing — Drinks, food and treats

Caring — Choosing favourite foods for baby/visitor/alien

Taking turns — Passing plates, pouring juice

Being helper; being a guest — Waiting, saying 'thank you'

Communicating — Talking with all the people at tea

Social

Appreciating — Taking responsibility Being 'in charge'

Gaining satisfaction — when 'guests' have a lovely time

Empathising — with guests who might be timid

Overcoming fears and worries — Trying new tasks — phobias reduced

Being able to stay near another person — Tolerating sitting beside a child

Emotional

from: *Play for Children with Special Needs*, Routledge © 2010 Christine Macintyre

house corner they will happily anticipate preparing to have friends to tea. While the children will share and offer plates willingly, they may have difficulty with gripping and releasing small items such as teaspoons, and understanding one-to-one correspondence could be tricky. However, placing one cup on one saucer is a good way to help them understand. After experiencing this, asking, 'We have three people coming to tea, how many cups will we put on the table?' and gradually building the demand is useful practice.

Children on the autistic spectrum may have great difficulty visualising what is going to happen, because they lack the imagination to anticipate 'tomorrow'. Asking them to do so could cause unnecessary stress so their practice can best happen on the day of the party. They may also find difficulty tolerating sitting beside other children at table, but these competences are important for everyday living and if they can be learned, then, for children with severe impairments, real progress has been achieved. Perhaps asking one child to offer a biscuit to just one other child can be a starting point for learning to share. Mums and dads will tell the kind of biscuit the child prefers and that can make a big difference!

Most children will enjoy baking. Make sure the wooden spoons are large enough to ease gripping and if the butter/margarine is hard, providing resistance, then the mixing action will strengthen hands and arms that have poor muscle tone. The children will learn to count spoonfuls and to follow a picture recipe. On the recipe card, single words, e.g. 'Stir' or 'Mix', can help whole word (look and say) recognition and can be spoken while accompanying the action.

Children with dyspraxia, with ADHD, and perhaps most of those with other learning differences need to focus on the planning and organising as well as doing the tasks. They will be able to imagine the party but find difficulty in knowing what to do first, and then next and what comes after that. The children could make a plan setting out questions, e.g. who will come to our party? When will it be? Where will the guests sit? And so on. Preparation of sandwiches with spreading and cutting gives very good practice in coordination at the midline of the body.

Children with dyspraxia generally have difficulty with directions, so tasks such as 'Put one plate on the table in front of each chair. This will help you to set out four places for our guests' are helpful. Once this has been achieved, ask the children to set the saucers or plates without the chairs indicating where they should go. (Observe each child's spatial awareness.) Allow them to move round the table to set it, for they will not be able to visualise 'opposite' settings.

The organisation also can be highlighted in the clearing away and tidying up process, asking, 'What shall we do first? Let's look for unfinished drinks that might spill. Carry these cups carefully to the sink.' This event planning is also helpful for children with ADHD as the sequence is spelled out and they are actively engaged in all the tasks. Success, of course, is always followed by overt or covert praise.

Mathematical development: setting the table

In setting the table, stress 'four people will come to tea' – or two people, depending on the children's competence and experience. Then ask, 'How many cups will we need? Can you put them on the four saucers? Please put a spoon on each saucer.' The children should count out four – or two spoons. This develops one-to-one correspondence and is a highly visible activity. Moreover, it has a purpose in getting the party ready. There is also the possibility of emphasising transfer of learning from one situation to another, e.g. when you can do this, you will be able to help set the table at home and perhaps you could help Gran at her house too? Many children with learning differences find this difficult, so gentle explanations and looking for ways to explain transfer always help.

Then, from a bundle of spoons, ask the children, 'Please give me one/two/three/four.' This is very difficult and needs to be built up slowly, but it does show whether the children have grasped the meaning of numbers. Many children with Down's syndrome will happily count from 1 to 10 and enjoy that achievement without really understanding what the numbers mean.

Action songs that stress numbers are helpful, e.g. Five little buns in a baker's shop.

Ideas for developing language and literacy

Many children who have hearing difficulties are strong visual learners so key words can be written on cards, clearly articulated by the teacher and the children can be encouraged to repeat them when they show interest in trying to do so. This should not interrupt the play but if the children are willing to listen to one or two clear repetitions of just one or two words, they will be more likely to want to repeat them.

Decide where single words on cards could be placed/emphasised to encourage speaking, e.g. TEA, CUP, SPOON, SUGAR, CAKE.

Encourage the children to enjoy a matching game with one word and matching picture (Figure 4.1), then two and so on, building up numbers so that there are alternatives. Then the children have to make choices.

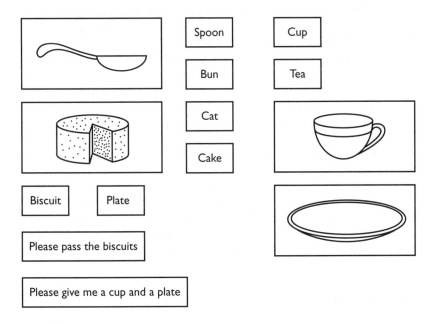

Figure 4.1 A matching game

Later, develop these same words into sentences. Then take some words away and let the children replace and speak their chosen words:

Please may I have a . . .? Where is the . . . for the sugar?, Please pour . . . in my cup.

Once the children recognise even one word, they can place it on the table in the correct place. Select an action song, such as 'I'm a little teapot', to encourage them to role-play in this game.

Organisational phrases can be helpful too, e.g. cards with 'Please pass the biscuits' or 'Please give me a cup of tea and a plate'.

As soon as possible, children should experience counting out items, e.g. 'Let's put three biscuits on the big plate.' The number 3 can sit on the table to prevent forgetting 'how many' are required.

Supporting children with Asperger's syndrome in the house corner

The key aim is to help children to turn-take in conversations and to use appropriate speech (not pedantic or overly repetitive speech).

Allow the child with Asperger's to speak a practised statement or question to initiate the conversation, e.g. 'I love coming to tea parties. Is there cake for tea?'

Children with Asperger's syndrome will probably need some preparatory thinking through the events so that they understand what will happen. Following Carol Gray's advice on using social stories, the following might be useful directly or as a template for other stories. She advises that the story should have four types of sentences:

1 *Descriptive*: Say where the situation occurs, who is involved and why.
2 *Perspective*: Describe and explain the reaction of others in the situation.
3 *Directive*: Say what the child is expected to do or say.
4 *Control*: Develop strategies to help the child remember what to do or understand the situation.

It is important that there are enough descriptors otherwise the story becomes a list of instructions. An example of a social story for the house corner might be:

Today we are going to have a tea party in the house corner (*descriptive*). The children will be excited because they have been invited, just like you (*perspective*). It would be lovely if you could say, 'Thank you for inviting me to your party' (*directive*). Everyone will sit down at the table and wait for Jake because he is the birthday boy (*descriptive*). There will be a birthday cake with four candles and you can help Jake to blow them out (*descriptive/directive*). Everyone will sing 'Happy Birthday' in quite a loud voice (*descriptive*). Be very calm and wait till the song is over before you leave the table (*directive*).

And for children with autism, one key aim might be for them to tolerate another child sitting near and staying in place to have a piece of cake.

The social story could be shortened:

It would be nice if you could sit down at the table (*directive*). Tom wants to sit in the chair next to you. He is kind and wants to be your friend (*perspective*). Stay quietly to see the birthday cake. It will have candles (*directive/descriptive*). All the children have to wait sitting at the table to get their piece of cake (*directive*).

These stories should explain what is going to happen. Other children know routines intuitively. The stories explain how the child should behave and hopefully ease the child's stress in encountering a new situation.

Other house corner events

Of course, preparing a tea party is only one of the many scenarios that the children will envisage or be invited to join in the house corner. Others might include:

- getting ready for a celebration (Christmas, Diwali, the Chinese New Year, Guy Fawkes, Halloween or whatever is meaningful to particular children/cultures). One group watched a video of part of the Edinburgh Tattoo and then developed marching games. This helped their spatial awareness, rhythm and timing (counting March, 2, 3, 4 and Halt, 2, 3, 4) as well as encouraging them to 'walk tall'. Some played imaginary bagpipes and a group built their own castle!
- Important home events can be rehearsed too and these can prepare children for changes in their usual routines. Many children with learning differences need detailed support with changes that other children welcome. Practices, e.g. stroking a fluffy toy, can help them recognise the amount of strength needed when tending a pet. The transfer should be explained (see 'Sensations' in Appendix 7).

Other useful experiences might include:

- welcoming a new baby home (why baby will need Mum's attention; how Mum will need help from her special grown-up child; what tasks the child can do; how helpless the baby will be; why the baby will cry; where the baby will sleep, and so on);
- having a new pet (why the pet will feel strange and timid at first; how to be gentle when stroking the pet; choosing a name; why the pet has to sleep in a basket, and so on);
- mum going to into hospital (getting better; Gran coming to stay; visiting and coming home again; busy nurses and doctors taking away pain; having medicine; having special treats, and so on);
- decorating a bedroom (choosing colours; having a cupboard for toys to live in (to remove distracters from view); where to buy paint; what equipment will be needed; what fun it will be painting the walls, and so on);
- understanding the bathroom (having a shower, using the toilet, tolerating the flush, adults locking the door – all these experiences can be frightening and explanations and pretend practices can release stress and increase tolerance).

Intellectual

Understanding that clothes can change characters — Role-playing

What shall I be? — Decision-making

Will the costume fit? — Problem-solving

Taking part in dramatic play, e.g. being a fireman — Acting

What resources will match my costume? — Planning

Movement (motor)

Dressing and changing clothes — Fastening buttons, zips

Using resources — Floor mop (Cinderella), tutu (ballet dancer)

Making resources — Crowns, necklaces, wands and other props

Learning in the dressing-up corner

Social

Listening to their wishes — understanding perspective — Assisting others to dress up

a) In waiting for a costume
b) In building a drama sequence — Turn-taking

That characters change, and altering motivations to suit — Understanding

Someone else's ideas/plan and giving praise — Following and adapting ploys

Emotional

Having confidence — a) to join in b) to become someone else and take on their role

Empathising

Understanding different roles

Avoiding suppressing fears — by acting them out in a safe place

Gaining satisfaction — from taking on another preferred role

from: *Play for Children with Special Needs*, Routledge © 2010 Christine Macintyre

Scenario 2 Supporting children with learning differences (SEN) in the dressing-up corner

This is usually a very popular corner as most children enjoy taking character parts and carrying out their roles (Figure 4.2). The items can suggest more adventurous ideas than the house corner – in fact, aliens and all sorts of creatures can be created. The box should have a variety of items that can lead to imaginative play, e.g. long scarves and pieces of coloured material that can be adapted to suit many imaginative games. 'Outfits' for firemen or nurses have their place too. These are especially useful if stories or specific teaching is linked to a meaningful event in a child's experience; perhaps if one child has to go into hospital, stethoscopes and bandages can help allay fears of new situations through learning that nurses and doctors are there to help, not frighten, children, or if there has been a local fire, then children can enact the parts the brave fireman play. But items like these can actually inhibit imaginative play because they suggest that there are correct things to do and behaviours that match the chosen costume. However, they can stimulate play in children who are afraid of venturing into the unknown. Similar restrictions can come from having kilts or saris, although they can help cultural awareness. So providing a balance of items that develop skills in contexts or titillate the imagination so that children can go beyond where adults go, is best.

Figure 4.2 Dressing up

Resources need not be expensive. Large cardboard boxes stimulate many games, especially if they are large enough for the children to go inside. They can also provide welcome shelter for children with ADHD or autism who find the setting too busy and threatening. In the box or the homemade tent they can have some time alone. And although a selection of resources can be stimulating for some, others can be over-whelmed by having too many things to choose from. However, crawling into the box gives children time to observe others and watch their ploys, hopefully building their confidence to come out and try.

Children on the autistic spectrum who find difficulty in understanding their own role are very unlikely to be able to understand dressing up and adopting another character, and this is very hard to explain. The children could also be distressed by seeing familiar faces and bodies 'disappear'. Probably children on the spectrum would not choose to be involved; this is why having choices is so important.

Children with Asperger's syndrome may want to join in and could benefit from learning to speak as the characters do. In so doing they may find ways of adapting their speech because they are naturally pedantic. Adapting to a new character is something they will probably have to rote-learn, so they need more time and more detailed explanations that other children do.

Children with dyspraxia are likely to be intrigued with the idea of dressing up and their lively imaginations will be stimulated. However, they will probably have diffi-culty donning and fastening up their costumes. Tabards are easily made and can be decorated by the older children. They can be easily slipped over the children's heads and so don't delay the play. Making them wide with long pieces of Velcro fastening ensures that they fit many children. So they are very useful additions to the box. (For ideas about making costumes, see Macintyre and McVitty (2003).) A definite benefit for children with dyspraxia is the extra practice in planning what to wear and then selecting and donning appropriate garments – hopefully in the correct order.

Adopting another character can be ideal for children who are a little dissatisfied with their own. Children with ADHD often recognise how their impulsiveness upsets others but they do not know how to change. Perhaps 'becoming someone else' and acting as they do could help them find the way?

Scenario 3 Learning through outdoor play

It goes without saying that safety is a prime concern here – for all children, but espe-cially those who may be overly impulsive and do not have the inbuilt safety mechanism (often referred to as 'angels looking out' for them) that usually develops two weeks after children learn to crawl. So setting up the equipment needs careful planning. The children learn so many valuable lessons about controlling their bodies through learning to balance on different pieces of equipment, and muscular activity increases their strength. This is a real bonus for those with poor muscle tone. The children's endorphins will also be activated, releasing the 'feel-good factor' that can lift spirits and last throughout the day. And as more and more researchers are finding strong links between gross motor skills and classroom learning, not just for the confidence move-ment competence brings but also for the useful pathways in the brain being confirmed, the importance of movement has been given a huge boost. Findings such as that chil-dren who didn't crawl may later have handwriting problems, recognising that the

Intellectual

The sequence of actions — Planning

Equipment and resources — Organising

Remembering what comes first then next — Sequencing

Completing the action — Doing

Estimating distances/heights — Judging

Knowing when to jump, throw, chase etc. — Timing

Movement (motor)

Balancing — on benches before and after jumping

Coordinating actions, control — Slowing down and stopping at the correct time

Transitions — Joining two actions together

Gross motor skills — Crawling, climbing, walking, running, jumping, rolling*

*pencil rolls only for children with Down's syndrome

Outdoor play on large apparatus

Social

Learning to let others go first (developing understanding of how others feel) — Waiting Taking turns

Watching others; copying good ideas on seesaw — Cooperating

Ball skills, e.g. throwing/catching/aiming — Being part of a team

Matching movements; fitting in spaces — Making up a movement game in twos

Emotional

Paying attention — Remembering and carrying out instructions

Gaining confidence — Becoming motivated to try more movement sequences

Endorphins working

Releasing tension/energy/stress — Running, jumping, wheeling

Reducing cortisol — Calming down

from: *Play for Children with Special Needs*, Routledge © 2010 Christine Macintyre

crawling pattern sets up a template in the brain that eases further learning and that the climbing pattern is the same as the crawling one, justify giving children lots of time to play on apparatus outside. Furthermore, moving like this and achieving movement challenges are what most children want to do!

Making decisions about the arrangement of the apparatus is important. There must be space between pieces so that the run-up to one does not cross the landing space for another and there must always be room for children 'to catch up with their feet' or even tumble over without impeding others. It is also best if the arrangement considers the timing and effort required to master different pieces. So a balance activity that needs control, e.g. walking along an upturned bench, should come after a quiet, sustained activity such as crawling through hoops; it should not follow a 'fast' activity, e.g. jumping down from a climbing frame, because there might be momentary disorientation. The same applies to taking a moment after trampolining. Finishing this kind of activity needs time and space to regain stability or even just a moment to catch one's breath!

Then the apparatus should house different levels of challenge so that able and less experienced children can all develop their skills. Having ladders inclined at different levels on the climbing frame would be an example of this. Also it is good to consider 'escape routes' so that children can change their minds if they feel they have over-estimated their ability. For jumping down can look easier from the ground than from being up there, especially if other children are waiting for a turn. Large mats underneath climbing apparatus are essential.

Observation and assessment

The transitory nature of movement makes assessing it difficult. This is easier if apparatus is arranged in a circuit, for this allows staff to follow a child round different pieces of equipment to note where difficulties come. Staff also need to check whether children avoid certain pieces – this can be very revealing. Wondering why Jordan would not walk on the 'wiggly worm' that was really a chalk line drawn on the grass, the staff observed him around the circuit and they noticed that when he balanced along a bench, the child's toes were turned in (his hips and knees were turned in too) and that made changing direction difficult.

Drawing out an apparatus plan (Figure 4.3) and writing the developmental competences alongside shows whether the circuit (a) has a balanced approach, i.e. is not all running and jumping, and (b) whether specific children will be able to find enough activities to match and challenge their current status.

Children with cerebral palsy can walk underneath a suspended ladder, reaching and grasping the rungs as they go. This will help to release spasm, achieve a bigger range of movement in the joint and strengthen the affected limbs as well as letting the children know they are being included. Even walking (with support where necessary) across a thick mat gives them another kind of experience. It is important to give balance and strengthening opportunities whenever this is appropriate.

Many children on the autistic spectrum will love to run and jump and climb. Some appear fearless, so careful observation regarding choice of activity is important. Just recently one child, severely affected by a 'nearly related to autistic condition', showed improvement after horse riding. Did the effect of losing and regaining balance contribute to this effect? Certainly Charlotte Moore talks of her boys 'being lit up by

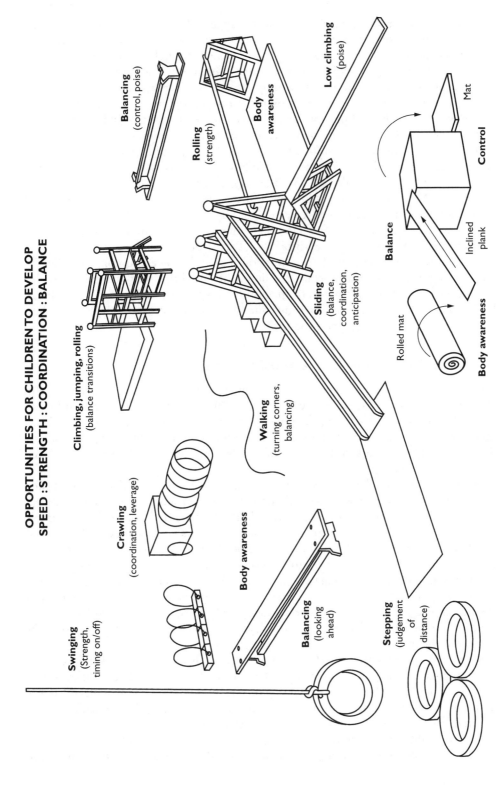

OPPORTUNITIES FOR CHILDREN TO DEVELOP
SPEED : STRENGTH : COORDINATION : BALANCE

Swinging
(Strength,
timing on/off)

Crawling
(coordination, leverage)

Climbing, jumping, rolling
(balance transitions)

Balancing
(control, poise)

Rolling
(strength)

**Body
awareness**

Low climbing
(poise)

Body awareness

Balancing
(looking
ahead)

Walking
(turning corners,
balancing)

Stepping
(judgement
of
distance)

Sliding
(balance,
coordination,
anticipation)

Rolled mat

Body awareness

Balance

Inclined
plank

Mat

Control

Figure 4.3 Example of an apparatus plan

bouncing' on the trampoline. Would it be possible to have a trampoline with safety netting in the setting? It seems strange to omit any possibility of improvement and often large local stores can be persuaded to fund such a purchase. It's worth a try.

Children with Down's syndrome who have short limbs and quite a stocky build may not be keen to try but activity can 'get things moving' apart from the essential strengthening benefit activity brings. Gradually introducing low-level equipment rather than them being overwhelmed by large pieces can give them the confidence to try.

It is very useful to stress the planning and organising components of movement, especially for children with difficulties (primarily dyspraxia, ADD, ADHD – but arguably all the other learning difference conditions too). Just asking the children, 'Tell me what you are going to do' or, after the action, 'Tell me what you planned, was it successful? No? Then how could you adjust it next time?' These are all useful interactions that show if the children can plan! Of course they need the language to be able to do this. One teacher who had taught one child a star jump was surprised to hear him explain, 'I'm going to do a big fly.' And he did!

For children who do not wish to venture onto even the lowest equipment, rolled up mats offer a safe alternative. They can lie on or crawl/roll over the mats and this experience lets them see the world from another perspective, so provides a valuable, if basic, source of learning. And if all the children, whether active or not, learn to love being out of doors, that can be good too!

Scenario 4 Learning in the music corner

Involving the children in using percussion is an excellent way to develop their sense of rhythm, their fine motor skills, their listening skills and their tolerance of different sounds/noises, quite apart from helping them appreciate musical sounds and learn about pitch and tone. Handling the percussion improves dexterity and gripping, e.g. the triangle or the beaters for the tambours; it also helps finger mobility and the development of the pincer grip.

Having children involved in rhythmical activities gives staff a wonderful opportunity to observe and investigate why many children cannot keep a beat. In the activity shown in Figure 4.4, the teachers found that the children who could not replicate a simple rhythm were the ones with learning differences. Was this because they could not hear the rhythm? Certainly this links with Peer's (2002) finding that youngsters later found to have dyslexia lacked discriminatory hearing. Her study concerned phonics and children's difficulties in learning to read, but possibly this lack hindered their development of rhythm too? Certainly in the early years, these children did not enjoy nursery rhymes or keeping the beat in action songs. And of course hypersensitive-to-noise children might have difficulty tolerating cymbals and maracas, so these could be omitted or be introduced gradually.

Rhythmic activities are so useful for children with dyspraxia too and children with cerebral palsy can enjoy the sounds and handle small tambourines and beaters with ease. Such practices also help coordination at the midline of the body with two hands doing different things. In twos, the children can enjoy making 'conversations' with different pieces of percussion and this helps turn-taking as well as giving enjoyment.

Gradually the children come to appreciate that sounds can suggest happenings, e.g. a cymbal and soft beater can suggest thunder, while short sequences of different sounds

Intellectual

Rhythm   Learning

Different qualities   Accompanying
of sound

Different instruments   Recognising

the beats   Counting

the different instruments   Naming

words of songs   Planning

the number of instruments   Organising

Movement (motor)

Playing   Different instruments

Controlling   sounds

Coordinating   Two hands doing different
things

Two hands doing the same
things (cymbals)

Controlling   length of sound

Accompanying a dancer

Learning in the music corner

Appreciating   Tone

Understanding   a) that black notes are symbols for
sounds

b) how sounds can represent ideas,
e.g. fire crackling, rain pattering

Playing together   Cooperating

basic compositions   Sharing

to others making sounds   Listening

for instruments   Caring

within the group about   Talking
the sounds

Investigating   Different sounds and how they
can make sound story

Responding   to sounds

Gaining confidence   in playing and listening

Social

Emotional

from: *Play for Children with Special Needs*, Routledge © 2010 Christine Macintyre

Figure 4.4 Children using African drums

can accompany a dance or simply suggest moving (shaking tambourine) and 'stop' (a beater making one sharp sound). This develops listening skills.

All this can be done in addition to playing 'real' music. Many children with learning differences can be soothed by familiar pieces of music and of course strong rhythmical music can accompany dances the children have composed. Descriptive words can enrich vocabularies and the children often enjoy making up words to describe the sounds.

Playing the piano

Although playing the piano seems to have fallen from favour nowadays, I have found this activity very useful for children with dyspraxia. They enjoy having immediate feedback from the sound and are intrigued by playing just one scale. Although tucking the thumb under the arch to allow the flow of eight notes is quite a challenge, they love to try and when they find this pattern can be replicated at different points on the keyboard, they learn about high and low sounds as well as how to make them.

Observing how the children play is revealing too. If they thump the keys, it shows that the proprioceptors in their fingers are not relaying information readily enough. The children thump to make them work harder! These are the children who will have to sharpen their pencil all day long because they have pressed too hard, so helping them understand the difference between pressing the keys lightly and thumping them is really beneficial well beyond the musical experience. And of course learning short

Intellectual

Beach/golf course | Where is sand used?

Egg timer (fine sand) | Timing
Measuring/estimating
Spades of sand | Counting

Choosing correct tools
for the job | Selecting

Empty; full | Language
Heavy; light; overflowing
More than; less than | Properties of
sand

Wet/dry/runny sand discussions, e.g.
a) is it easier to run on | Discussions
wet or dry sand?
b) what kind of sand is
best for building?

Movement (motor)

Gross motor
manipulative skills | Using spoon/spade
to fill bucket or tipper
truck

Fine motor | Decorating the sandcastle

Patting | Building castles in a pail

Smoothing | Making sides firm

Finger | Making pathways in wet sand —
strengthening | ruts

Coordination at the midline of the
body; control in building/pouring
water

Learning at the sand tray

Making a moat | Cooperating
in building
roads together

Carrying water and pouring
carefully to fill moat

Building roads and | Gathering resources/
making a village | discussing plans

Letting more children
join the game

Sharing plans and
developing ideas together

Appreciation | of effort needed to build

Tolerating | feel of sand; getting grubby

Visualising | the bigger plan, e.g. imagining
living in a castle

Empathising | with the hard work
builders do

Social

Emotional

from: *Play for Children with Special Needs*, Routledge © 2010 Christine Macintyre

Intellectual

Building a cave that won't collapse; or a paper boat that will float in the moat

Learning about floating and sinking

Problem-solving

Dry and wet sand — selecting and adapting

Estimating levels; pailfuls needed

of water/ice/freezing melting disappearing

Understanding changing properties

Displacement of water when blocks are added to the tray; submerging

Floating and sinking   Investigating

Movement (motor)

Placing   small world figures

Controlling   water flow in filling/emptying tubes, syphons

Building   wet sand; strengthening hands, arms and shoulders

Developing coordination at the midline of the body

Learning at the water tray and sand tray

A day at the seaside   Discussing Anticipating

A sandcastle with a moat   Cooperating to build a scene

Splashing water Scattering sand   Looking out for others

Ideas and equipment   Sharing

Enjoying   the feel of water at different temperatures

Splashing, swirling, mixing colours

Making firm sandcastles

Creating   'miniatures' of real events, e.g diggers

Appreciating   ideas and developments

Social

Emotional

from: *Play for Children with Special Needs*, Routledge © 2010 Christine Macintyre

pieces that use few notes give the children something to 'show off' and so helps their confidence, especially if their parents don't play!

An important finding is that the fingertips are connected to a large piece of tissue in the frontal cortex of the brain (Winkley 2004). This is the problem-solving area so the old saying that 'musicians are good at maths' may be correct after all!

The chapter finishes by giving three more analyses, and this pattern can be followed for all areas and activities.

Scenario 5 Learning in the water tray/sand tray

Example 5, 'Learning in the sand corner' is analysed on the photocopiable resource pages here but practitioners are given the opportunity to discuss how and why amendment should be made for the children in their particular setting.

Scenario 6 Learning in the garden area

It is to be hoped that many centres providing for children with learning difficulties would have access to a garden of some kind, but perhaps this is not the case everywhere. Practitioners are free to discuss the analysis for the children in their particular setting if they do have a garden area.

> Have you heard of special needs?
> Things like ADD?
> 'Dys' conditions – lots of them,
> Well, they're all part of me!
> It seems I am 'co-morbid',
> Now that's beyond the pale
> For if you sweep aside the labels
> You'll find ME – an alpha male!
> At school I do get 'special' help,
> It's due to me, I'm told,
> to compensate for being slow,
> But Mum says I'm pure gold!
> So what if I don't have some friends,
> I love to play alone,
> For no one runs as fast as me,
> Especially going home!
> Christine Macintyre

Intellectual

Vegetables/fruit/flowers — Recognising plants in the garden

Sizes of plants — Comparing
Speed of growth

Providing food — making fat balls, bird bath/table — Attracting birds and mini-beasts to the garden

Learning about poisonous plants — deciduous plants

Safety in garden equipment — Safety issues

Keeping the garden tidy/ free from litter — Responsibility

Learning what fruits/veg. will grow — and what dishes they will make, e.g that chips are cut-up potatoes! — Fruits Vegetables

Movement (motor)

Planting — bulbs and following their growing cycle

Watering — Carrying a watering can

Pouring — the water gently so as not to disturb plants

Stepping — gently to avoid damaging the plants

Controlling — Scattering seeds carefully

Covering — delicate plants with fleece in the winter

Learning in the garden area

Collecting conkers to see the prickles (to keep the seed secure) — Collecting seeds together in the autumn

Preparing a patch of soil — Working together

Plants and seeds for tubs — Choosing/discussing

Taking care of a plot together — Having responsibility in twos or threes

Social

Appreciating — how beautiful plants are; how delicate plants are

Watching — the process of seeds maturing and growing

Tending — Watering, feeding, supporting plants

Observing — Slow growth — delayed gratification

Emotional

from: *Play for Children with Special Needs*, Routledge © 2010 Christine Macintyre

Chapter 5

Understanding the learning process as children play

As the earlier chapters have described, play-/child-centred learning should be an activity based on the children's maturational stage and natural desires and to encourage development (remembering this has four fields, i.e. social, emotional, motor and intellectual). Learning opportunities and activities have to begin where the children are and then enhance that status in a positive, timely way. As Donaldson (1978) attests, 'Teaching is not about children acquiring a series of skills – learning should always develop in a meaningful (to the child) context.' So numbers can best be learned by looking at road signs and buses, on the counters in shops and on mobile phones!

But how *do* children learn? And why should some find learning so much easier than others? And how can learning through play facilitate further learning?

These are difficult questions, for how do we know if or indeed when children have learned something and whether this experience has been easy or difficult? We can only know by observing the children carefully and noting any changes in what they can do or what they communicate by gesture or by words, while the ease or difficulty can only be gauged by the amount of focus or concentration the children display and possibly by the quality of the finished product. But as we know, highly significant play scenarios may have no product at all, for the idea of having to produce something was never the stimulus for imaginative play. So to record progress, the process must be observed (see Table 5.1). The process of learning is a well-used phrase. But what exactly does it mean?

Children make their learning explicit through their gestures and actions and, if they have speech, through their explanations. If there is absolutely no change in these, has there been any learning? And while children are able to learn without overtly moving, can they play if they are still? If learning is problematic, professionals, e.g. GPs, teachers, physiotherapists, occupational and language therapists, try to find what part of the learning process is causing the problem and put strategies in place to help the child overcome what is wrong or, at the very least, they try to appreciate and monitor the learning differences that lead to difficulties in meeting the academic, social, emotional or motor norms that allow children to cope with the activities of daily living at home and at school.

Table 5.1 Observing the process of learning

Things that can usefully be observed	Key aspects of development
How children organise themselves, their resources and possibly their friends	Intellectual, Motor, Social
How children make plans and adjust these as the play goes on	Intellectual
How children use their imaginations as a basis for new thinking	Emotional
How children involve others and share resources; take turns	Social, Motor
How children move effectively and efficiently as appropriate (using fine, gross and manipulative movement skills)	Motor
How children speak with other children and adults in a meaningful way, perhaps one that explains plans or suggests ideas that expand the play	Social, Emotional, Intellectual, Motor
How children focus for an appropriate length of time (NB. If a narrow focus continues too long, it *might* signify obsessive behaviour)	Intellectual
How children gain confidence; show pleasure in continuing the process; treat others respectfully	Emotional

Play as learning, play as practice

One of the never-ending discussions about play is very often based on this dichotomy, i.e. are children at play learning new skills or 'only' practising known ones? Can adults trust children to find a balance between the two so that the learning pace is just right for them? For most children the answer must be 'yes', for they have a strong intrinsic motivation to learn and do more. They won't stay with what they already know. If anyone doubts this, watch any young child. They are rarely still and even at 3, constantly ask, 'Why?' and persist till they are satisfied. However, some children lack this intrinsic urge and it can be very hard to find ways to motivate them even when imaginative resources are provided.

This is particularly apparent in many children with Down's syndrome. When the children reach 5, many 'change from being relatively able problem-solvers to become increasingly reluctant learners' (Wishart 2006). This can be seen when they adopt counterproductive strategies to avoid learning. They will give the teacher a hug – and who can resist them? Then the teacher realises that the child's social strength has caused her to abandon her lesson! Sometimes they gesture quite firmly they have had enough, or if they have language, a favourite delaying tactic is to promise 'later!' But whether they have Down's syndrome or not, it can be very difficult indeed to persuade a reluctant child to learn.

So how do children learn? What is involved in the learning process?

When children learn something, they take in information from the environment through their senses; that information travels through the central nervous system to

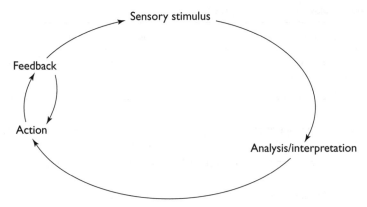

Figure 5.1 The continuous chain of learning

the brain for analysis and a lightning instruction is then sent to the correct part of the body and this promotes the action or outcome. If this cycle is efficient, learning should be straightforward, but if there is a breakdown at any stage or if the children have not gained the neurological maturity to cope, i.e. if they are expected to do more than they can, their learning will be compromised.

The cycle explains the mind–body link. For although all learning takes place in the brain, the body acts as the vehicle that transmits the information from the senses to be analysed in the brain, and once this is done, it acts to show the effect. But before it can do this, it must take information from the senses. Isn't it fascinating that the less well-known senses, i.e. the vestibular or sense of balance, the proprioceptive sense that promotes body awareness and the kinaesthetic sense that enables us to make spatial judgements, are the fundamental ones that enable children to move with confidence and competence? For how could we discern learning if we couldn't see children move? Sometimes these three senses are clumped together and are known as the sixth sense! That stresses the importance of the three that work together to tell us where and how we are functioning in space. This ability is the cornerstone of further learning.

So a continuous chain involves sensory stimulus, analysis/interpretation and then action. There must also be feedback from action and stimulus, and efficiency depends on all parts of the chain functioning well. Ideally, there will be a feedback loop from the self-evaluation of the action that will provide the key to improving the next try. Children with dyspraxia don't appear to have this skill. As a result, they become tired and frustrated by not knowing what is causing them to repeat mistakes and not improve what's wrong. Lack of feedback also hinders the transfer of learning from one situation to another.

Sensory stimulus

The senses are part of the nervous system. The sensory receptors take information from the external environment through seeing, hearing and feeling (i.e. through the visual, auditory and tactile senses and those of taste and smell) and from the internal

Table 5.2 The stimulus to the learning process

The senses	Their key role	Indicators of difficulties
Vestibular	Balance	Unsteadiness; unwilling to leave the ground or take risks
Kinaesthetic	Spatial awareness	Unable to judge distances; bumping and spilling.
Proprioceptive	Body awareness	General clumsiness in both gross and fine motor skills
Visual	Seeing and tracking (functional sight)	Squinting; rubbing eyes; holding a book too near or far from the face
Auditory	Listening and hearing	Distractibility; inability to focus
Tactile	Feeling and touching	Needs firm touch or can't bear to be touched. Intolerance of materials, textures. Feels pain when hair/nails cut
Taste and smell	Accept/reject food	Unwilling to try foods; upset by smells; possible psychological barrier to eating

environment (e.g. the pain receptors, the urges that prompt action, and the sixth sense (i.e. the vestibular, proprioceptive and kinaesthetic senses)) and they transmit this information to the brain. Within the brain there are relay centres that send the input to the correct part of the brain for analysis.

The senses all act together (i.e. sensory integration), stimulating the learning process (Table 5.2). So a clear understanding of the senses and the parts they play in perceiving the world is so important, for if that first stage is inaccurate, the whole cycle could be distorted. One example of this could be when the children suffer from visual stress (previously called Mears-Irlen syndrome) and are misled by distortions of text and/or distressed by light sensitivity. A second could be seen by the effect of the temperamental trait 'impulsiveness' that makes many children act without considering alternatives or even working out the implications of their actions. This keeps adults on the alert, for most young children are impulsive rather than reflective, are they not? Children tend to become more reflective as they mature, i.e. when they gain the experience to allow them make comparisons and when they appreciate that others might feel or prefer to act differently from themselves.

The vestibular sense

The vestibular sense, which controls balance, is the leader of the sensory orchestra. All other sensory information passes through the vestibular mechanism at brainstem level before that information can be processed accurately. The vestibular is the first sense to function and even in the womb it is important in getting the baby in the head-down position ready to be born. From then it controls any change in posture or alignment and so keeps us steady as we carry heavy loads in one hand or jump across puddles or onto buses. More subtly, it helps ascertain hand and foot dominance, which is important in writing, kicking a ball and in most activities of daily living, for not having a dominant hand or foot can cause confusion and delay in responding to instructions. Practitioners, not appreciating this, might think the child did not understand or was not able to do the set task and give unnecessary repetition instead of helping them to develop dominance. This is frustrating for everyone!

Difficulties/observation points indicating a poor vestibular sense:

- A poor sense of balance. Children stumble and knock into things.
- Motion sickness. They avoid roundabouts and could be car sick.
- Dislike of quick changes of direction. Children will follow a rounded path but avoid the sharp changes of a zigzag one.
- Difficulty in focussing – easily disoriented.
- Difficulty in staying still.
- Difficulty in crawling using the cross-lateral pattern.

The vestibular system could be compared to having an internal compass that tells us about directions, e.g. forward, up, down, sideways, and allows the body to adapt in a controlled manner.

The kinaesthetic and proprioceptive senses

These two names are often used interchangeably. However, to be accurate, the kinaesthetic sense only comes into play when there is muscle contraction, i.e. when the body is moving. The proprioceptive sense, however, works all the time, even when the body is at rest. Both senses relay positional information. The proprioceptive sense is linked to body awareness and can be stimulated by games such as 'Simon says' or for the younger ones by jingles, e.g. 'Tap Time' (see Appendix 7) and old-fashioned games such as 'the Hokey Cokey' or 'In and out the dusty bluebells'. These activities help them know where the different body parts are in relation to one another. The proprioceptors are all over the body and in the muscles and joints. Receptors are even located in the hair follicles and literally tell us where we end and the outside world begins. So children with a poor proprioceptive sense often have difficulty being still – they have to move so that their kinaesthetic and proprioceptive senses provide them with more secure information about where they are in space.

Difficulties/observation points indicating a poorly developed sixth sense:

- A poor sense of poise, e.g. the child who has to slump over the desk. (Make sure the feet are supported on the floor and that the desk is the correct height. Try brief spells of walking/sitting with a beanbag on the head to give the feeling of pushing up against gravity rather than giving in to it.)
- An inability to crawl using the cross-lateral pattern. This is a very important skill and should be practised every day.
- Easily tired by the constant effort needed to stay erect. (Have very brief spells of activity interspersed with rests. Make sure asthma/diabetes tests have been done.)
- Constant movement and fidgeting. (Provide a beanbag to sit on and something to squeeze.)
- Poor depth perception causing stumbling or 'falling over thin air'. (Check that the flooring is plain, as patterns can distort vision, giving false cues.)

- Poor sense of direction (rehearse 'where to go' and draw a simple map to show cues, e.g. a picture of a door with 2 on the door – ahead of the child having to find this place independently.)
- Poor body awareness. (Play 'Simon says' types of games, remembering that after 'Heads, shoulders, knees and toes, knees and toes', you can extend this by adding 'heels, bottoms, back, and nose, backs and nose'! This uses the stretching up time very usefully, for how do children wipe at the toilet if they don't know where their backs are? (More rhythm ideas can be found in *Jingle Time*; see Appendix 7 and the bibliography.)
- Difficulty in gauging own strength. This can occur if a child hits another, or 'if things just come apart in his hands', or if he tears the paper when practising his emergent writing. (Often, discussing the effects of squeezing clay using different amounts of strength can alert a child to differences in cause and effect. Also, the jingles, e.g. 'Smoothly, smoothly stroke a tiny kitten', in Appendix 7 can give practical experience of the effect of using too much strength).

The visual sense

Assessing vision should cover much more than distance vision, which is often the main concern in a simple eye test. Children who 'pass' this may still have difficulties tracking, i.e. following the words on a page or the writing on the board. Functional vision depends on maturation of the central nervous system (CNS).

Visual–motor integration skills are as important as distance sight. The two eyes have to work together to focus on an image (convergence). Some children with poor convergence will see double images that confuse letter recognition; others will see the letters move on the page and may endure severe eyestrain trying to adjust to the movement. This is Mears-Irlen syndrome (or visual stress) and can be helped by coloured overlays or coloured lenses in spectacles. Children also benefit from being allowed to choose the colour of paper that suits them best because different colours defeat the reflection of light. They also prefer reading non-justified print (Barrington Stokes publishers in Edinburgh produce books on cream paper with non-justified print).

Children must also be able to adjust their focus so that they can decipher objects and print from different angles and directions. This is called accommodation. The three skills, convergence, accommodation and tracking, are all prerequisites for quick identification and reading fluently without strain.

Difficulties/observation points indicating a poor visual sense:

- poor reading ability due to discrimination/tracking difficulties;
- child explaining that letters jump or overlap on the page;
- child moving the book around 'to catch the letters';
- rubbing eyes or partially closing them to keep out the light;
- distress at being asked to read aloud;
- difficulty following written work on the board;
- handwriting sloping in different directions;
- poor letter formation.

The auditory sense

During the first three years, the child is listening and learning to tune in to sounds of his mother tongue – and thereafter it is harder to adjust to the tenor of another language. Obviously, loss of hearing significantly affects learning, but children who 'can hear' may have auditory discrimination problems and these may be the basis of a recognised additional learning need, e.g. dyslexia or dyspraxia. If the child cannot hear the difference between 'p' and 'b' or 'sh' and 'th', then both reading and spelling are impaired. Even silent reading is affected because then the child listens to an inner voice – if the sounds are not clear, then this process will be affected just the same as in reading aloud.

Hearing too much (i.e. auditory hypersensitivity) can cause as much difficulty as not hearing enough. Children bombarded by sound can have difficulty selecting what they need to hear from the variety of different noises around them. Even in a quiet classroom, some children find hearing the teacher difficult, as they cannot cut out minor rustles and squeaks. One child refused to go on a class outing to the pantomime because she anticipated not being able to hear the words from the stage for rustling sweet papers and popcorn!

Sounds are transmitted to the language-processing centre in the brain. The right ear is the more efficient. Sounds heard there pass directly to the main language centre in the left hemisphere whereas left-eared children have to pass the sound to the language subcentre and then through the corpus callosum to the left hemisphere for decoding. This very slight delay may put left-eared children at a disadvantage.

Difficulties/observation points indicating a poor auditory sense:

• easily distracted;
• over-sensitive to sounds;
• poor sense of pitch and tone;
• confusion in distinguishing letters;
• slight hesitation or longer delay in responding;
• not hearing questions clearly affecting responses;
• constantly asking for things to be repeated.

The tactile sense

Being touched is one of the earliest sources of learning and communication, and touch receptors cover the whole body. They are linked to a headband in the brain called the somato-sensory cortex that can register heat, cold, pressure, pain and body position. It makes an important contribution to the sense of balance.

Some children have a system that is over-reactive to touch and this causes them to withdraw or be distressed by hugs, i.e. responses that most children welcome. This can make them isolated and peers can mistakenly interpret their reactions as snubs. Yet these same children can be 'touchers', seeking out sensory stimulation through contacting others even though they themselves would be distressed by such overtures. Tactility or sensitivity to touch is also important in feeding. Some children cannot bear spoons to enter their mouths and much prefer finger food that they can cope with on their own.

The pain receptors can cause difficulties too. Some children are hyposensitive and may not feel pain or temperature change – they may have a huge tolerance to holding hot plates or going out-of-doors ill clad in icy winds. And the hypersensitive ones will over-react about injections and visits to the dentist because they are supremely painful. Some even feel pain when having their nails or hair cut and some cannot tolerate seams in socks. All kinds of problems arise from being hypo or hyper touch-sensitive.

Difficulties/observation points indicating a poor tactile sense:

- Dislike of being touched, so withdrawing from contact.
- May be a compulsive toucher.
- Pain may not be registered appropriately, causing over- or under-reaction.
- Poor temperature control.
- Allergies – possibly eczema.
- Dislike of contact sports/games.
- If the child lacks protective control, he may not sense danger.

The senses of smell and taste

The sense of smell is the most evocative of the senses as it can stimulate memories, e.g. of a garden visited long ago or a hot summer when the milk turned sour! The sense of smell can also stimulate the hormones controlling appetite, temperature and sexuality. Certain smells can become associated with different situations, e.g. the smell of a hospital can conjure up memories of pain; the scent of flowers can recall a happy event such as a wedding or a sad one such as a funeral. It is controlled by the thalamus.

Some children and adults are much more odour-sensitive/intolerant than others. Some associate smells or tastes with colours or have difficulty entering a hospital or dentist – not because of anticipating pain but because of the acrid smells that often linger there. Soaps and perfumes can have the same effect – sometimes leaving practitioners baffled as to why they have been rejected! The sense of taste depends on the sense of smell so it is not difficult to understand why children often refuse to accept new foods because they do not like the appearance or the smell.

However, some of the earliest learning comes through these senses, as during the sensori-motor period the baby will put everything to the mouth. This most sensitive part of the body will tell about the taste and the texture of the object and whether it is hard, soft or malleable as well as whether the taste is pleasant or not!

Difficulties/observation points indicating a poor sense of taste and smell:

- Children may be very faddy about new foods and only tolerate a very restricted diet.
- They may refuse to go to the bathroom because of the smell of antiseptics or even of scented soap.
- They may dislike being near other people, especially if perfume or after-shave can be smelt.
- They may be upset by floor polishes or other chemical sprays.

Although the senses can be studied separately, they do support each other by working together. More and more with the research into dyslexia, it can be claimed that we 'read with our ears' (Peer 2002) as inability to distinguish different sounds hinders recognition of single sounds and blends in the written text. A poor sense of smell also inhibits the ability to discriminate different tastes. This is the basis of sensory integration, e.g. hearing the approaching bus lets me judge the speed and allows me to get ready to alight even before I see it. However, the balance needed to alight smoothly without stumbling (i.e. dynamic balance) can be affected if the visual sense does not complement the vestibular one. This is why sensory integration is often called cross-modal transfer. Reactions may vary according to the type of stimulus, its intensity, its rate and its duration. Most people can only tolerate a shrill sound such as a fire alarm or an intensive light for a short time without distress and many children on the autistic spectrum have this hypersensitivity impacting on their living all day long! So any signs of distress must be investigated by considering how the children are receiving and interpreting their sensory input.

The second part of the learning cycle concerns the analysis of the sensory information in the brain. Studying the brain is a vastly complex endeavour and the notes in this text just provide some introductory information.

The human brain is made up of many parts each with its specialist function, e.g. to turn sounds into speech, to memorise events, to let us understand others, to make us happy or sad. But each brain is unique, constantly changing and very sensitive to its environment. Each of the parts is interdependent and interactive and, especially in the early years, children's brains are flexible. Their functions are not fixed. Sometimes one part can even take over from another to compensate for trauma. But this plasticity disappears with maturity and it becomes harder for one part to compensate for difficulties in another, e.g. in instances where a stroke inhibits the language centre in an adult's left brain, the right side, with time, effort and specialist support, can learn to produce speech. It is unlikely, however, that the cadence (highs and lows of intonation that give speech its rhythm and often meaning) will be retained. But the key effect, returning speech, is the all-important gain.

So brains are at their most plastic during infancy but firm up as maturation occurs. During this time they alter according to the activities, experiences, illnesses and traumas they encounter. By the time we are adults our mental landscapes are so individual that no two adults will perceive the same events as being the same (Carter 2004).

Brain activity is controlled by electric currents and chemicals. The different parts are bound together in a dynamic system of connecting networks that interact to allow us to do many things at the same time. This activity is so complex that the brain may never fully understand itself (Winston 2004). The cells within the cerebral cortex are neurones or grey (thinking) cells and glial or white cells. There are billions of thinking cells that communicate with one another through their axons and synapses. Even more numerous are the glial cells that support the network. They protect and feed the axons and generally keep the network in good working order.

One neurone firing alone would have a minimal effect. It would not even succeed in twitching an eyelid, but one neurone excites surrounding neurones and patterns of activity are formed. And as these patterns fire repeatedly, stronger pathways or templates are formed and laid down in the procedural memory. This is Hebbian learning and explains why repetition or practice is the way to establish skills and also why we don't forget skills like riding a bike. Some children, especially those with dyspraxia and other specific learning difficulties, don't have this ability and must learn skills as a first-time try. It is not difficult to see how this can cause delay and how it impacts on forward planning and organising.

Even when the brain appears to be idle, e.g. during sleep, there is a pattern of constantly changing activity, and when someone takes on a complex mental task the whole cerebrum lights up. New connections are made with every incoming sensation and old ones disappear as memories fade. Certain patterns of speech production are so strongly inherited that only an abnormal event can disturb them.

During foetal development the brain develops at the upper end of the neural tube that forms the central nervous system. The main sections of the brain, including the cerebral cortex, are visible within seven weeks of conception and at birth the brain holds as many neurones, i.e. about 100 billion, as it will have as an adult. The neurones, however, are not mature, for many axons are unsheathed by myelin (i.e. the insulation that allows signals to pass along them) and there are few connections between neurones. Large areas are only minimally active at this point – only the brainstem (controlling the rate of breathing and blood pressure), the thalamus (allowing response to touch) and the cerebellum (stimulating movement and muscle tone and relaying messages to the correct part of the brain for analysis) are functioning well.

The uterine environment has a profound effect on the wiring of a baby's brain. Babies born to drug addicts are frequently addicted at birth and some illnesses such as German measles in the mother can affect both hearing and sight in the unborn child. On a lighter note, babies born to mothers who eat curries often enjoy spicy foods best. The male foetus has genes that stimulate the production of testosterone and this slows the development of certain parts and speeds others. Boys are generally slower at fine motor skills such as writing because the language centre in boys is myelinated later than in girls but they are ahead in spatial orientation tasks and direction-finding. If the male foetus does not receive enough testosterone, the brain will remain more typically female and if a girl is exposed to a male-pattern hormonal sequence she will have traits more usually defined as masculine. Baron-Cohen (1991) advises that autism is, in effect, 'too much maleness' and is researching the effects of a surge of too much testosterone in the early stages of pregnancy.

Inside the developing brain, neurones or thinking cells race about trying to form a network with other neurones. If this doesn't happen, the cell will die and, due to a process called apoptosis, will be washed away. This ruthless pruning of the dendritic arbour is to strengthen connections in the developing brain and rid the brain of superfluous ones. Unfortunately, this process may wash away potential gifts – it has been mooted that in Down's syndrome there is too much pruning. This process is called apoptosis. As one example of this, photographic memory is quite common in very young children but is a skill that is lost in pruning. Incomplete apoptosis (being left with too many connections in a specific area) may account for the gifts of mono-savants.

The timing of the maturation of the brain is interesting. We don't remember much before the age of 3 years (prodigious memories are one sign of giftedness in children) because the hippocampus, the brain area that lays down conscious memories, is not mature. Emotional memories, particularly negative, fearful ones, however, may be stored in the amygdala, which is functioning at birth. Another theory suggests that in children with autism the amygdala is shaped differently, altering its function and causing it to store too many negative memories.

The frontal lobe kicks in at 6 months, bringing the start of cognition. By a year, children are able to rationalise and make choices. If they are shown two toys they will make a choice rather than trying to grab both and they recognise that objects that are out of sight do not really disappear. Myelination gradually creeps upward and outward. The parietal lobe allows the development of spatial understanding and enjoyment of games such as peek-a-boo shows that elementary turn-taking is understood.

The language area becomes mature around 18 months. The area that deals with understanding (Wernicke's area) matures before the part that produces speech (Broca's area). There is a time when toddlers understand much more than they can say. This can lead to frustration in them not being able to make their needs known, possibly one cause of the terrible twos.

As myelination moves to the frontal lobes, the child develops self-awareness but these lobes do not become fully mature till adulthood. This is why adolescents are much more emotional and impulsive than adults and why young children may be less aware of the effect of their actions on others. If children who bully others have delayed myelination, could it be that they are unaware of the hurt they cause?

The third part of the cycle, the outcome of learning, forms the content of Chapter 4 when the learning potential in play activities is explored. But, of course, being able to participate depends on the first two parts of the cycle functioning effectively.

This brief chapter is to support practitioners as they observe difference and difficulties and to give them confidence in making judgements about if, when and how to intervene in children's development and when to ask for expert help. It also suggests a variety of ways in which this might be done.

Knowing oneself: enhancing self-esteem

The most important development of all comes in children developing self-knowledge and, through that, building a positive sense of themselves. If they have a positive self-esteem, then they seem to develop a much more encouraging attitude towards living as well as learning and they seem able to ward off slights and disappointments much more readily than those who are ambivalent about who they are. They become resilient children rather than vulnerable ones. And as children build their self-esteem as they grow, adults and other children, through their interactions, play a major part in its formation. This is vitally important.

So what is self-esteem?

Self-esteem is the evaluative part of the self-concept, which is a global picture children build of themselves through the reactions they receive from others, especially the significant ones, i.e. parents, teachers and peers in their environment. Children build this picture first of all when they are egocentric and at this stage it is not evaluative. The children do not compare themselves to others. So this is a critical time for positive attitudes to be formed. Then gradually the children become aware that other children are not the same as they are and they begin to recognise that these others have different perspectives, outlooks, family structures, gifts, talents and learning differences, and perhaps the children would prefer to be as they are. This is the beginning of self-esteem and it is firmed up as the children grow and recognise the responses others give to them in their environment.

The children's reactions to what they see as their 'lot' – and whether they are pleased or not – are influenced by two major sources. The first is their inbuilt or inherited temperament. Whether the children are 'naturally' extrovert or shy, impulsive or 'slow to warm up' is down to what they have inherited through the gene pool. Of course, they can learn to behave in different ways, i.e. to be more outgoing or energetic, but their temperamental traits will to some extent influence how they see their world and evaluate their place in it. And in times of stress, they are most likely to revert to their natural pattern rather than using the learned one. This is further complicated by meta-incongruence, i.e. occasions when verbal and non-verbal communications do not agree. Then the children are confused to be told verbally that they have done well when the teller's more powerful body language conveys disappointment or even distress. Parents will be able to relate to this when perhaps they are waiting for a diagnosis in hospital. Although their overt communication says to the child, 'chin up, it will be all right', their tense shoulders and rigid posture signal intense anxiety and fearfulness. And as 90 per cent of the meaning in a message comes through the non-verbals, children pick up these conflicting signs very readily.

The second depends on the three Rs, i.e. respect, relationships and responsive care. From the earliest days when children bond with their parents and family, they are being established in a warm, supportive environment that provides security and comfort. Children with a very different start, who are neglected and abused, may grow up defensive, afraid to bond and make friends because of anticipated worries about what might happen if they lay themselves open to relationships that turn sour. That said, many children overcome horrific situations and do well, but when respect and responsive care are absent, this is so much harder.

But what about children with learning differences that often lead to their having difficulties meeting the 'standards' or 'norms' that have been set by some statutory body? Even in the most respectful environment the children know they need more time, more repetitions or specialist help. It is their right to have this, but often there are financial or other hurdles in the way. But well-supported children, no matter what their differences are, must be enabled to have high self-esteem. How could this come about? How can adults help children to do the following:

- approach new learning with confidence?
- express their true feelings without becoming over-emotional?
- cope with changes in routine?
- cry without feeling this is a weakness?
- recognise that they can win respect by being kind to others and realising that those others have worries too?
- value what they have and keep any difficulties in proportion?

This last 'wish' has been achieved by head teacher Margaret Pope (1988). She explains, 'Telling a child he is good at something when he knows full well he's not, far from raising his self-esteem, only diminishes it.' She continues, 'I have been amazed how well children respond to an acceptance of their difficulties when this is coupled with positive suggestions that can lead to improvement.'

These positive suggestions have to be designed for each child, recognising their uniqueness and what they want to achieve. One suggestion is for children to be helped to list things they are good at. Again, this depends on adults being able to analyse what competences each child has and what aims are realistic. But even making small achievements overt can instil confidence – items such as:

I am good at getting up early.
I help Mum clear the table without fussing.
I am good at tidying my books away.
The little ones in school like me.
I always find the car keys for Daddy. He is pleased.

This strategy has been tried out successfully with many children. It was found to work best after some special teaching input on the importance of caring for others. The activity was the same for every child although the lists of competences varied. There were added bonuses as the activity went on. Once children felt secure through knowing that they had had the potential to succeed in small things, they were able to share ideas about what they would like to be good at next and this helped determine realistic, shared targets.

One important piece of research by Gurney (1987) deserves current consideration. He advised, 'Teachers, praise yourselves! Teach the children to praise each other then teach the children to praise themselves!' So each day, teachers can recap and say, 'Haven't we done well today – we have learned three very important things! We have all worked together to build this collage with no squabbling. That made everyone happy. Then everyone was allowed to play at break and no one was bullied. Everyone was smiling, no one was sad, so I think this must be the best class in the whole school.'

Focussing on personal qualities like this allows each child to feel they *can* succeed. A final note also recalls Paley's (2005) finding that giving children more time engenders calm and reduces stress. Then more children are allowed to play. Surely the best way to support children is to show them that the most important kind of learning can be achieved by them all. And guess what? It might even be fun!

Down's syndrome

Children with Down's syndrome face many problems in growing up and these impact on their family members too because the children will always need a great deal of patient and appropriate support if they are to fulfil their potential. If this is given, plus screening and any necessary medical intervention, then the children can surprise by what they can achieve, even if this takes a bit longer than with others. So the best advice is to be positive and to understand what is causing the children's difficulties as a basis for planning interventions. This process, of course, will require to be amended according to the observations that pinpoint each child's specific profile of support needs.

What causes Down's syndrome?

Down's syndrome is a chromosomal disorder caused by the presence of all or part of an extra chromosome and this leads to over-expression of certain genes located on it. This causes the physical, intellectual and health differences and difficulties that typify the condition. The condition is often called trisomy 21, i.e. children have three rather than two copies of chromosome 21, and 95 per cent of affected children have this type. It is a congenital condition that most often occurs before conception and can be identified before or at birth. Trisomy 21 is caused by a meiotic nondisjunction, meaning that a cell has not split correctly, and when it duplicates, the error is passed into the daughter cells. All cells in the body have 46 chromosomes except the sperm and the ovum, i.e. the gametes, which should have 23 each. When they fuse to form the zygote, the chromosomes from the mother and father come together to make up the 46. But in Down's syndrome, the gamete (i.e. either the sperm or the egg cell) is produced with 24 chromosomes and so the embryo has 47, with three copies of number 21: 88 per cent of cases come from the maternal gamete and 8 per cent from the paternal one.

Children with mosaic Down's syndrome form a much smaller group, i.e. 3–8 per cent of all cases. Again the condition is caused by an accident in cell division but this time within the embryo. The timing of the accident will determine the number of cells that are affected. If it happens early, perhaps at the four-cell stage, then more cells will have the characteristic 47 chromosomes. If it happens later, then the effect is determined by the pattern (mosaic) of cells that are affected. However, if trisomy 21 has already occurred, i.e. if the *embryo* has Down's syndrome, a further nondisjunction means that some cells are likely to revert to a normal chromosomal content, so this is beneficial. While it is not really helpful to talk in generalisations, children with mosaic Down's syndrome tend to be intellectually less impaired by their condition; they have perhaps 30 more IQ points – but this is not always the case. Some children with trisomy 21 will do better than some with mosaic Down's; and other, environmental factors impact on development too.

A third but even less common type is usually called translocation Down's syndrome (also called Robertsonian translocation or familial Down's syndrome), occurring in 2–3 per cent of affected children. The parents are phenotypically normal but in the embryo the long arm of chromosome 21 is attached to another, often chromosome 14. This condition does not show maternal age effect and is as likely to have come from the father as the mother.

How many children are affected?

In 2008 the numbers of children with Down's syndrome were calculated as 1:730–1,000 children and the condition occurs in all ethnic groups and across all social classes. It is a random accident, not due to parental behaviour or environmental circumstances.

Is the mother's age a contributory factor?

The statistics can be quite confusing, for the greatest number of affected children are born to mothers under 35, but that is because there are many more children born then. However, the mother's age does play a significant part:

> Mothers in the age range 20–24 have the probability of 1: 1562;
> At 35–39 this increases to 1:214 and
> Above age 45, it is 1:19.
>
> (Wikipedia)

Prenatal screening

There are different screening techniques that can discover Down's syndrome. In some regions these tests will be carried out as routine or alternatively they may be done where non-invasive tests indicate possibilities of the presence of the condition. If the result is positive, the parents are left to make the choice whether the pregnancy should proceed. In some areas the test is not possible on religious grounds. Amniocentesis and other tests such as chrionic villus sampling (CVS) do carry a very small risk of mis-carrying a child. In a very few cases (0.06 per cent), a foetus that has been diagnosed as having Down's syndrome may not be affected at all, but false positives are rare.

What are the birth signs?

The characteristics that alert the paediatrician or midwife are immediately apparent at birth although not all need to be present for the diagnosis to be made and some can appear in children who do not have Down's syndrome.

The baby is likely to be quite small and certainly floppy or hypotonic, i.e. lacking muscle tone, so careful physical support is needed for longer than for neurotypical children. This poor tone means that the motor milestones will be delayed, but the children do learn to sit and walk and run – just a bit later and often with rather a clumsy gait.

A common but not unfailing characteristic is found on the child's hands because there is a single palmar crease (also called the simian crease) across one or both palms and one fissure on the pinkie. There also will be a larger than usual space between the first and second toes.

The facial features have indicators too. The child's head can be rounded with the face rather flat; the ears are small and low set. The eyes have an almond shape due to epicanthic folds at the corner of the eyes and this gives a slanting appearance. There are white brushfield spots on the iris but thankfully neither the folds nor the spots affect vision. That said, most children with Down's syndrome will require spectacles for short sight at around 7 years of age. Very often the child's tongue protrudes and parents can find this really distressing. There are three reasons for this. The first is that the oral cavity can be small so that there is not enough space; the second that the tongue may be thick at the root, making eating messy and articulation difficult, and the third is the general poor muscle tone that hampers control. But as this improves with maturation and practice, e.g. chewing, strengthening the muscles in the mouth, most children can learn to keep their tongues in.

A small number of children have cervical instability. This means that pressure on the vertebrae in the neck may cause the (sometimes weaker) bones to dislodge, compressing the brainstem. Practitioners should always and immediately check with the parents whether this is the case for their particular child and at all costs prohibit any activities that stress the neck, e.g. forward or backward rolls.

What are the key concerns?

The first consideration must be the children's health, for while many do enjoy good health, many more have some or even all of the problems listed below. These include:

- health difficulties, e.g. heart, thyroid, gastrointestinal tract problems, leukaemia, ear and chest infections, short-sightedness;
- physical difficulties due to their body build and low muscle tone, e.g. gross motor clumsiness and poor fine motor coordination;
- intellectual difficulties due to difficulty and even reluctance in mastering 'the key cognitive skills of childhood' (Wishart 2006), e.g. in learning to read, write and count.

That said, however, children are affected to different degrees. Some have severe heart problems such as tetralogy of Fallot, a condition where the structure and therefore the function of the heart are impaired (this can be identified prenatally). This needs surgical intervention. Some children have minor problems while many have none. It is also true that many slight cardiac problems self-correct without intervention.

Thyroid problems need careful supervision in their own right and because they can exacerbate heart difficulties. As a result of thyroid inefficiency many children develop dry flaky skin, which can split and become infected. Gastro-oesophageal reflux or gastrointestinal atresia (blockages) make feeding and retention of nutrients difficult and lack of fluid can cause problems with constipation. Obstructive sleep apnoea can cause choking.

Some children are more prone to ear infections than others and this affects their hearing and necessitates time off school to have grommets fitted. Tests of hearing acuity are essential as if the children don't hear the sounds of their own language at the correct time (due to poor discriminatory hearing), they may never speak, or if they do, their articulation may be unclear. This is why a visual curriculum is a must.

Children with Down's syndrome have an increased risk of some types of leukaemia although many do overcome this.

There are some health bonuses, e.g. less chance of developing diabetic retinopathy and fewer dental caries. Also, children with DS are less likely to have epilepsy or if they do, the condition tends to be less severe and is amenable to medication. Moreover, a supportive and resourceful environment, while not 'curing' Down's syndrome, can contribute greatly to a positive outlook. The expected lifespan has greatly increased too although more adults than in the neurotypical population do develop dementia.

Social development

Having Down's syndrome is not all disappointing news, for the enchanting sociability many of these children display may be the result of a gene effect linked to the condition (Arron 2006). This is a definite bonus and assures children of a welcome and friendships in school. This gives them a wonderful start. With inclusion now the norm in many regions, children's language skills also improve. Also, because the children's differences are readily recognised by others, parents and other children can empathise and offer support.

Moreover, there are no traits such as poor behaviour associated with the condition, although children at 4 may exhibit the tantrums of the 'terrible twos'. This is an expression of their delayed development rather than incipient, long-lasting aggression. The expectation is that the children are functioning two years below the norm but of course the range of ability is wide and each child must be assessed carefully.

Many children with Down's syndrome, even those without spoken language, are good communicators and the other children, recognising their condition, are likely to be patient and help them. While this has many plus points, the children must be encouraged to be independent and develop life skills of their own. Often they will stand and allow others to do what they could manage for themselves, e.g. in getting dressed or in fetching resources in class. The same kind of well-meaning over-care can come from parents and practitioners/classroom assistants who intervene too much, making the children dependent rather than independent. Getting the balance right can be tricky. And of course the children can play on this. As one mum explained, 'Having a disability doesn't turn them into angels!'

Intellectual differences: disappearing motivation

In the early years, progress can be encouraging, but for some reason this is not usually maintained and ongoing research is trying to find why. Wishart has found that the children may well be adding to their difficulties by opting out – 'Later' can be a favourite interjection! They may also use counterproductive strategies, e.g. turning to their teacher to give a hug instead of turning the page or completing their task – and who can resist their smiles? But in so doing they have avoided their reading, the puzzle or whatever it was they had to do! Strangely and unexpectedly, the avoidance doesn't appear to relate to success or finding a task too hard. The children just 'switch off'. This tactic could be one of the steps that move children from being relatively able problem-solvers to being reluctant learners. Motivational deficits can greatly add to the cognitive difficulties, for if the children are not willing to try, it is hard to make progress.

Yet children can thrive on social tasks and enjoy role play even if they do not have language. They always understand more than they can say, so parents and teachers have to avoid speaking in language that is too simple. That said, repeating one action word at a time, e.g. 'down' as the child goes down a step, can help the development of their speech. Hopefully the child will copy the single word, then adding the child's name could be the next step, e.g. 'John is down.'

Some regions employ PECS, i.e. the picture exchange system that gives non-verbal children a measure of independence and communication, while others prefer not to use signing or PECS in case the child depends on that and doesn't make the effort to speak.

The brain of Down's syndrome children

In Down's syndrome, the cerebrum is less complex than in other children. Paediatricians describe their smooth brains as 'having embryonic simplicity'. This means that there are fewer gyri and sulci, and so less room for complex messages to connect. Also, in apoptosis, i.e. the dendritic pruning that happens in the first months, children with Down's syndrome appear to lose too many connections. The hippocampus, the memory area, is also reduced in size, explaining the need for over-learning and repetition.

There are also fewer neurones or thinking cells to make connections to other cells. So, the stimulus received from the senses, i.e. the first part of the learning cycle, may take longer to have an impact. In children with poor muscle tone, it is vitally important to build up the myelin that surrounds the axon as this acts as insulation, allowing the messages or instructions to pass along a direct route. Myelin is built up when the children are active, so play and freedom out of doors are very important for the generation of strength.

Teaching children with Down's syndrome: a visual curriculum is a must!

The key words in planning learning activities are 'concrete materials, hands-on experiences, a visual curriculum'.

Reading

If hearing is a problem, the 'look and say' method of teaching reading is often successful. It is a good idea to have single-word cards with familiar known words, e.g. the child's name, Mummy, dog, etc. A photograph or picture helps the first step when the children place the word alongside the image. Then the photo can be taken away to check that the word has been retained. Once each word has been learned, the child can shuffle the cards to make a naming or a matching game and eventually the words can be built into sentences. Using words that will eventually occur in their reading books makes transition easier. The children love to have a real book just as their peers do. Gradually phonics can be introduced once the link between sounds and the written word is understood. The Down's Syndrome Association advises that the children should recognise around 50 words before the teacher begins to sound them out.

Comprehension is often well ahead of the ability to speak, so practitioners should choose stories/activities to match that level of attainment rather than depending on verbal responses.

Counting

In maths, the Numicon method allows the children to see and touch the equipment that builds patterns to clarify conceptual understanding of numbers. This is colourful and attractive and provides opportunities to develop fine motor skills as well as visual and maths ones. Fine motor skills can be rather clumsy due to the different patterning of the palmar crease, so developing hand mobility and careful placement (control) is an added bonus.

Some rote learning can be enjoyed, e.g. the children love to count out loud from 1 to 10, or even higher, but the numbers can be spoken without any real understanding of what they mean. If in doubt, practitioners can have a bundle of crayons or small items and ask, 'Please give me two' or 'Please put four apples in the basket' and check the response, rather than assuming that counting correctly means understanding the concept of number or the relationship between different numbers.

When following the more usual classroom methods, number lines need to be clearly marked and directions repeatedly explained, whenever possible linking movements to the concepts, e.g. 'let's go up three stairs, then through the door'. Difficult concepts such as 'more than' are very sophisticated and should not come before the basics, e.g. big/small, up/down, are clearly understood.

Movement programmes

Many children with Down's syndrome are not keen on PE, partly down to their rather stolid build, but activity is so good for their health and it is important that they feel part of their class programme. An activity such as rounders where the pathway is clearly marked is a good 'team game', and even if they miss the ball, they can run to the next station. Apart from being good fun, this game helps them understand directions and distances. Often their digestive systems can be sluggish and exercise like this can get things moving. Apparatus should be carefully chosen, e.g. in throwing and catching practices, large but soft balls and airflow balls travel more slowly and give the children more chance of success. The children enjoy 'Beat your own score' types of games rather than team games where rules are confusing.

Other games

Like all other children, they like to win, so this should always be possible! Simplified games such as dominoes or card tricks help the recognition of numbers and reinforce counting while board games such as snakes and ladders or ludo help counting, planning and sequencing if they are played for fun.

Children with Down's syndrome can always continue to make progress. The key is to stay positive, to recognise and build on the skills they have, and to praise every small achievement.

Attention deficit disorder (ADD) and attention deficit hyperactivity disorder (ADHD)

Schooling should be a time when children enjoy learning and gain confidence from the success this engenders. Thankfully many, even most, young children, fitting the norm, achieve and prosper. But although children with ADD/ADHD appear 'normal' (i.e. with no obvious physical or social handicap), they have complex difficulties with a neurological base. They are not badly behaved although they are often blamed for being so; there is a physical and psychological cause for their restlessness or withdrawal from learning, yet they are often denied immediate understanding and support. They are very often seen as a disruptive element in class and so are constantly being chided for non-compliance. As a result, they neither enjoy school nor fulfil their potential there. Yet they can be of average, even above average, intelligence, their potential being hidden by the three key difficulties that detract from their learning. These are:

1   inattention;
2   impulsivity;
3   hyperactivity (less so in ADD).

These traits remain constant over weeks, months and years, significantly affecting the children's or indeed the adults' ability to cope. They are not one-off inappropriate responses, perhaps due to a change in circumstances or unusual stress.

Children with these conditions feel their emotions so strongly that they are impelled to act. This can appear as inappropriate, challenging behaviour. It is not caused by poor parenting; it is caused by the neurological differences that impact on their perception, concentration, memory, coordination and control. These last two are especially difficult for children who have the hyperactivity element added to the difficulties of paying attention and cutting out distracters in the environment.

The symptoms are apparent before age 7 and result in children with a normal intellect underachieving because they find it so difficult to concentrate on their work. Behaviour problems are much worse than could be expected given the child's parenting and environment and in the absence of other learning difficulties.

Children with ADHD can have a difference in one part of the structure of the brain. The caudate nucleus is a mass of nerve bundles that are concerned with the initiation and control of voluntary movement. The right-sided caudate nucleus is larger than the left side in children with ADHD and the whole is smaller than in neurotypical children. One of the bundles is called the striatum and this works to inhibit behaviour and sustain attention. It is also linked to the limbic system that controls emotions, motivation and memory. The corpus callosum, the band of tissue that joins the two hemispheres of the cerebral cortex, is smaller too. Impulses pass from the different sides of the brain through the corpus callosum. It is important that there is room for these interactions not to be impeded. The frontal part of the brain, where the problem-solving and higher-order thinking happens, is also found to be slightly smaller, providing fewer neurones to carry out critical functions.

Another difference is the lack of the neurotransmitter dopamine that helps the control of movements and thoughts. Neurotransmitters facilitate the passage of sensations across the synapses and help responses to be timely and appropriate.

The positive news is that there are treatments for these conditions, and the symptoms appear to reduce in adulthood. Medical assessment may lead to children having medication (usually methylphenidate/Ritalin). It acts at the synapse to prevent the reabsorption of the neurotransmitter back into the bouton. The aim is to try to control restlessness or inattention. This may take time to have an effect, however, and anecdotal evidence explains that the some children can appear zombie-like. In these cases, the medication is obviously not being well controlled or correctly administered. Many parents, not sure of the effects on their child, are understandably reluctant to try. This text is not advocating medication; it is simply presenting possibilities. Non-stimulant medicines are being developed now and it is hoped that they will be effective in calming the children without side effects. Some parents find that dietary changes can positively affect behaviour. They remove caffeine, found in chocolate, coffee and some fizzy drinks, in some cordials and sweets with artificial colourings. An 'over-the-counter' nutritional supplement containing omega-3 has also been found to help.

The names indicate that there are two distinct manifestations of this condition. The first, ADD, has the key 'symptom' of inattention. The children's poor concentration means that they don't follow the trend of a lesson and misunderstand the sequence of developments. They are likely to daydream and withdraw from the learning that is happening around them or be distracted by something else in their environment. If their memory is poor as well, it is not difficult to see how progress can be limited. The second, ADHD, indicates that hyperactivity is a severely disabling factor. This may mean that children are compelled to leave their seat and rush across the room, very often leaving disturbed others in their path. They find it almost impossible to keep still for a length of time – unless they are totally occupied and interested. Both conditions can house impulsiveness – children who shout out answers before pausing to think whether they make sense or who are bombarded by so many answers to a question that they fail to select the best one. The children lack control over their responses. It is not hard to understand why parents, teachers and peers find their behaviour baffling, irritating and often embarrassing.

As with other additional learning needs conditions, there are many variations and subtle differences to thwart professionals who wish to make accurate diagnoses and develop programmes to support children with ADD/ADHD. There is no blood test that will spot the condition; the best procedure is the careful compilation of a diary at home and one at school. Observations should concern:

- Antecedent events (what triggered the episode?)
- What was happening before the event?

- Who was present?
- Where did it occur?
- What time of day?
- How long did it last?
- How often does it occur?
- What is the outcome? e.g. is there a change in child's demands/amount of attention/attainment of goals?

Repetition of incidents may well suggest strategies that can avoid reoccurrence, e.g. changes in seating plans or shortening curriculum episodes.

Co-occurrence with another difficulty

Unfortunately, having one condition does not preclude children having a second. In research terms this is called co-morbidity. However, a less frightening term is co-occurrence.

Two-thirds of children with ADHD will have at least one other coexisting condition such as dyslexia or depression or acute anxiety. One common co-occurring syndrome is Tourette's syndrome. This can mean that the children display either the vocal explosions or noises or physical shrugs (often called tics) or both. As in the 'normal' population, a number of children with ADD or ADHD have developmental delay and need parental/teacher support for much longer than their peers.

How many are affected?

The numbers of affected children are similar to those having other disorders, i.e. 5 per cent of children are thought to have ADHD, with the boy:girl ratio being 5:1. Research shows that affected boys tend to be more aggressive, physically confronting their frustration, while girls have the predominantly inattentive form (ADD) and so, because they don't cause disruption in the classroom, they may be under-diagnosed (Learning Assessment and Neurocare Centre; www.lanc.uk.com).

Is it inherited?

There is a great deal of research showing that this is an inherited condition. Studies have found that 25 per cent of first-degree relatives, i.e. parents or siblings, also had the condition and that in 80–90 per cent of identical twin pairs, both children were affected. And if parents have one child with the condition, there is a 40 per cent chance of another child having it too. Some 40–50 per cent of children with ADHD have at least one parent with the condition.

Redefinition

In a more positive mode, parents and teachers are asked to redefine how they think of the children and/or describe them to others. Changes suggested by Corlett (2006) (psychologists, not teachers) are shown in Table A.1. They explain that the outcome of such a shift in thinking might be that the children 'become viewed as tireless,

Table A.1 Redefinition of children with ADD/ADHD

Negative first thoughts?	Positive alternatives
Being out of seat too much	Energetic and lively
Talking out of turn or calling out	Keen to contribute
Losing and forgetting things	Absorbed in own ideas
Distractible	High level of environmental awareness
Impatient	Goal-oriented
Daydreaming	Bored by mundane tasks, imaginative

imaginative visual thinkers – ones not averse to taking risks'. They anticipate that such changes will have a positive effect on teacher–pupil interactions and on the children's self-esteem.

Strategies to help:

- Be careful where the children sit in class – a quiet spot with panels may be necessary to cut out distracters. Sitting near a child who provides a good role model can be helpful.
- Try to ignore minor upsets so that the child's name is not always being called out. 'Catching him being good' is the best way, but it can still be very difficult for children to comply.
- Keep tasks brief except if the child is bright and thrives on complexity. In that case, short tasks can cause frustration. Gifted children can have ADHD, although this is rare.
- Try to explain the length of the task so that the children can visualise 'getting it done'. A large egg timer (often obtainable from the nursery) can give a visual indication of how much time a task will take or how much time is left to complete it, as '5 minutes remaining' can be meaningless to a child.
- Provide immediate feedback whenever possible – and vary the activities so that boredom doesn't set in. Give rewards readily to boost confidence.
- Allow chill-out time. Very often the children can feel pressures building up and they know how to deflate their energies if they are allowed to be private or to let off steam in a safe environment.
- Allow the children to use headphones that provide soothing music or white noise.
- Children may have little appreciation of cause and effect, so 'future rewards' as bribes to behave have little effect. They are slower to learn skills such as self-management/problem-solving/coping with change.
- Allow the child to sit on a beanbag – this allows a little movement. Also provide a squeeze ball or clay to allow hands to work while the child is listening. These strategies can aid stillness.
- Have a daily timetable on view with the breaks clearly marked.
- Try to give some advance warning of changes in routine or of teaching personnel.

Above all, teachers have to build a positive relationship with the parents and explain that you appreciate that the condition is neither the child's fault nor that of the parents. The parents are likely to be exhausted and sensitive to any seeming criticism. It is also vital that the child has the same set of rules and that he appreciates that home and school are working together to support him.

Children have poor appreciation of cause and effect – so threats do not work. School can be a hostile place. Children need supervised chill-out time. Significant improvement is possible for 90 per cent of children if managed well.

ADHD/ADD summary:

- ADHD is a complex neurological condition that results in children having significant problems with concentration, hyperactivity and impulsivity.
- There are two distinctly different kinds. The first has key factors of impulsivity and hyperactivity, the second (often known as ADD) predominantly houses inattention.
- Five per cent of children are thought to have ADHD, with the boy:girl ratio being 5:1.
- Boys tend to be more aggressive while more girls have the inattentive form and so may be under-diagnosed (Learning Assessment and Neurocare Centre; www.lanc. uk.com).
- Two-thirds of children with ADHD will have at least one other coexisting condition such as dyslexia or depression or acute anxiety.
- The children often have developmental delay and need parental/teacher support for longer than their peers.
- Children may have little appreciation of cause and effect, so 'future rewards' as bribes to behave have little effect. They are slower to learn skills such as self-management/problem-solving/coping with change.
- Medical assessment may lead to children having medication to try to control their restlessness or inattention. This may take time to have an effect and will need careful monitoring and adjustment.

An introduction to autism, Asperger's syndrome and teaching strategies to support the children

Autism is a lifelong neurological disorder that affects how children and adults experience their world. The condition is not likely to be apparent at birth and children may be 2½ or so before communicative difficulties are suspected and aged 4 before a formal diagnosis is made by a psychologist or paediatrician. Having their child placed on the spectrum is hugely distressing for all parents. Often they feel that 'inside this different child is our own – the wonderful one that we have lost' (parent of recently diagnosed child). They pray that their child will emerge from autism and search for the key. If Asperger's syndrome is the diagnosis, the children will be intellectually more able; they will certainly have language and a very small number will have a pocket of brilliance (mono-savants). They may also have the commitment that develops original creative ideas. It has been suggested that Darwin had Asperger's. Yet the social communication problems, possibly the obsessive behaviour and an inability to empathise with others (a theory of mind) are still part of the condition. These are sure to make the children 'different'.

The triad of impairments in autism as identified by Lorna Wing and used by the World Health Organization are:

- *social*: impaired, deviant and extremely delayed social development, especially interpersonal development;
- *language and communication*: impaired and deviant language and communication, both verbal and non-verbal;
- *thought and behaviour*: rigidity of thought and impoverished imagination.

Social difficulties

The most common phrase used to describe children with autism is that they will not hold eye contact. They turn away and this can be disconcerting for those seeking interaction. This is because the children see the complex, constantly changing expressions of others as totally confusing and meaningless. They cannot read the meaning that is conveyed by facial expressions or body language. And as 90 per cent of the meaning in a message is transmitted by body language, their understanding is severely diminished. Researchers have found that many tiny babies only scan the lower half of their mother's faces, so from the start their learning is different.

All children on the spectrum have impaired social development and this prevents them making friends. The children do not relate to others in a personal way. One able child on the spectrum, when asked, 'What is a friend?', replied, 'It is someone who carries your books'. Even when prompted, no personal characteristics were forth-coming. Some children on the spectrum, most likely those with Asperger's syndrome, *do* want friends but have no idea how to make friendships happen. Prompted by their parents, some will memorise friendly overtures but when these are said out of context, they can sound very strange and cause other children to go away, leaving them disillusioned and not understanding why their entreaties were rebuffed. Many children with autism will make no social overtures at all and so they become isolated. The children themselves may not appear to notice this lack and prefer to play alone because that is less stressful.

Language

Some children will have no speech; others will use pedantic speech or learned phrases that do not fit the situation; others (with Asperger's syndrome) may speak 'too much', unaware of the effect this is having on others. The children may have no speech or they may have the early sounds, 'Mumma, Dada', but then this disappears and the children may never speak again. This is so distressing. And even when the children do speak – and some will speak far too much – their speech is strange, pedantic, over-correct speech – which may only be recognised as strange on reflection after diagnosis. They do not understand idiom or sarcasm and everyday phrases are understood literally, e.g. 'Has the cat got your tongue?' can cause real anxiety about their own safety and an aversion to cats, or a sarcastic comment such as 'Don't hurry!' can cause a child to delay even more. How confusing it all is! Or when a disaster happens, a perplexed parent can say, 'That's just great.' It is not difficult to understand the confusion when the child, not appreciating the intonation, sees this as praise, an indication that the incident should happen again! This strange lack of understanding and the disappearing speech are the first and most common factors that parents share when bringing their children for assessment.

Some children later found to be autistic will have prolific early speech but much of this will be mimicked rather than made-up speech. It can be hard to spot the difference till strange utterances are spotted. Charlotte Moore explains that when her son was given a toy telephone, he did not volunteer 'Hello', as most neurotypical children would, but copied a previously heard phrase, 'Please replace the handset and try again later.' Some children will repeat learned phrases that sound all right in context, e.g. asking, 'What kind of car have you got?' But then the same phrase will be repeated minutes later when the question is no longer relevant. Furthermore, the child is not likely to wait for or even be interested in the reply!

When children talk like this, the reactions from others must make them feel very strange. Perhaps 'not understanding' contributes to their reluctance to interact with others? Children often withdraw and lose the speech they had. Perhaps when they reach 2½, the demands put on them overwhelm them to the extent that they retreat into their own, safer world?

Thought and behaviour

Adhering to routines, not realising that if adults are not present, they 'can't know' what is going on and so cannot take appropriate steps to stop it or develop it, children on the spectrum often have a rigid adherence to routine. Unchanging timetables structure their day. If they have a picture of what will happen in their day, then they can feel secure, but any deviations can cause real distress evidenced by screaming, aggression or withdrawal. Taken further, this routine may develop into obsessions that provide comfort to the child but bewilderment to the parents. These may last for months and suddenly disappear, and another obsession will take hold. In some children and adults with Asperger's syndrome, if obsessions are valuable to others, they can lead to high-level careers because of the combination of high ability and ongoing commitment. Temple Grandin, a famous lady with Asperger's syndrome, realised two things: (1) she felt calmer when she was held firm; and (2) she found communicating with animals easier than with people. This led to her designing cattle crushes so that animals could be calm as they received their medication, and she has lectured all over the world on this topic. But if the obsession is collecting used tickets and lining them up, or only tolerating certain colours to wear, then this doesn't happen. However, it is to be hoped that the children gain comfort from their obsessions and routines and that somehow they are filling a gap in their lives.

Differences like these can cause the children to be bullied and careful observation by teachers is essential because the children won't tell. Why not? Because they think they already know! They don't realise that if teachers or parents are not present, then they can't know! And if children try to tell, they may miss the personal part of the story that holds the key to understanding. This makes supporting them very difficult.

Children on the spectrum have a total absence of pretence and while this means they are truthful children without pride or envy, this lack also prevents any imaginative play. The children lack the imagination to deal with events removed from the here and now. As Jane Asher, President of the National Autistic Society, explains, 'We need imagination to remember yesterday and picture tomorrow.' People need to consider how disabling it is for children not to be able to do these things.

In the early years, it is revealing to watch autistic children playing with a toy. They may use it as a comforter or as a 'spam', i.e. something to whirl or flap, but they will not give the toy a personality or build a story around it. Teachers need to be vigilant to spot this difference when there are many other children to be cared for. The 'play' of an autistic child will be qualitatively different. It will be repetitive and depersonalised.

Assessment must consider both verbal (all autists have difficulties here) and non-verbal intelligence, which can concern activities such as completing jigsaws, understanding puzzles or sorting things into groups.

So there are profound implications for children diagnosed as being on the autistic spectrum and for their families too as understanding and support will be needed throughout the children's lives. And of course children can be more or less affected by the condition.

What causes autism?

Although several and sometimes conflicting theories (e.g. inherited 'faulty' genes vs brain injury during development vs too much prenatal testosterone) have been put forward, as yet there is not one agreed cause. The link to the MMR inoculation has been disproved. However, there is no dispute about the claim that the condition is neither caused nor exacerbated by poor parenting skills.

The increase in numbers of people being diagnosed is startling – the National Autistic Society claim a 45 per cent increase in the number of autistic children in a single year, giving 2,204 Scottish children in 2004 and of course many more in England due to the higher numbers of children there. It has been mooted that there are 125,0000 children affected by autism in the UK. In their study of the prevalence of ASD (autistic spectrum disorders), Keen and Ward (2004) found that in a single, relatively small health district, the number of recorded diagnoses had doubled over a four-year period. They explain this by referring to the current recognition of ASD in more able children and the work to identify the co-occurrence of autism within other severe verbal disorders.

The increase in part must be due to better diagnosis, but non-scientific reminiscence must prompt the question, 'Where were they all when I was at school? There were no children flapping and wailing in the corner then' (Charlotte Moore – mother of three sons, two with autism). Before this survey, the usual ratio given was 1:165; it is now 1:100 children and some areas say 1:49! The boys:girls ratio is 5:1 with the ratio 10:1 for Asperger's syndrome. Some families have a clearly inherited form of autism – and in these cases more girls are affected, but it is more usually boys who have the condition.

For most children on the spectrum, the environment is full of distracters that prevent them focusing and learning. For them, bright lights, loud noises and colourful toys can be very distressing. Their senses become overloaded and their coping strategy is to 'shut down' or to flap their hands in distress, to shout and scream or self-harm. Some parents have to watch their children regress till they are almost unreachable, and even in milder cases the parents have to change their expectations and learn different ways of bringing up their child. This is very hard; however, children on the spectrum are not envious, whining to get something someone else has. Free of any guile, they are often very good-looking. They are totally uninterested in the latest craze. They relate best to those who put no pressure on them. This is hard for parents and teachers who are anxious that they learn the social 'rules' that make life easier for neurotypical children.

No one knows exactly what causes autism and there is no cure. But improvements are possible and the earlier specific treatments begin, the better. Ongoing research is continuing to confront the condition so when the cause is eventually found, there may be more effective ways to improve the quality of the children's lives.

Table A.2 shows the differences in speech and communication across the spectrum.

Strategies to support the children's learning

The TEACCH programme (parents and schools working together)

The main goal of the TEACCH programme is to help children with autism grow up to attain maximum autonomy when they reach adulthood. This includes helping them understand the world that surrounds them, acquiring communication skills and the basic skills of everyday living, e.g. using a knife and fork, that will enable them to socialise with other people, and giving them (as far as possible) the necessary competence to be able to make choices concerning their own lives.

The major thrust is towards improving communication skills and autonomy to the maximum of the children's potential, using education as a means to achieve that goal.

Table A.2 Differences in speech and communication across the autistic spectrum

Asperger's syndrome (high-functioning autism?)	Autism	Profound disability
Speech communication		
Fluent but not flexible ('dictionary speech')	Restricted, pedantic speech. Made-up words – gobbledegook, but important to the child, who repeats and repeats them, often chortling with pleasure	No speech – noises and grunts
No understanding of idiom, sarcasm or jokes	Little comprehension	Silence
Little eye contact	Looks away (peripheral vision may give better focus)	May briefly hold gaze but not comprehend what is intended
May overwhelm others by talking at length about their own interests; they may not stop because they know that someone else's conversation may confuse them	Screams, whirls, cries when frustrated	
Non-verbal communication		
Cannot interpret non-verbal communication so misinterprets meaning	Bewildered by not understanding – may 'shut down' or 'crash', withdrawing into repeated 'stims'	Little understanding – may respond to careful handling
Intelligence		
May have high IQ, but more likely to be average	Much lower; early precocity may be memory of others' words rather than own sentences	May smile or be able to indicate unhappiness
'Islets of brilliance' may depend on obsession and eye for detail. No transfer of learning	Omits personal pronouns – 'I'	Sometimes appears to understand but is not able to respond
Prodigious memory for facts and objects; no personal detail offered	Restricted speech, covering own wants	
Comments correctly but inappropriately; doesn't realise hut because of not empathising with others	Doesn't say, 'Look at . . .' or share interests	
	May have immediate or delayed echolalia (repetition of others' speech, like an echo)	
Understanding		
By adolescence, will quet question own differences and may understand and explain condition to others	Doesn't realise own differences, or at least cannot convey the realisation	
May have a sense of guilt	No sense of guilt or duplicity; doesn't bear grudges. No sense of pride	Has emotions but doesn't understand the emotions of others

Table A.2 continued

Movement		
A strange, stilted gait is common	Little sense of danger seems to protect the children as they climb and swing	Motor milestones very delayed. Probable use of standing frames. All equipment needs to be padded. Easily disorientated by changing directions
Can take part in activities but the children have difficulty in following rules, e.g. changing ends in a game	Trampolining is a favourite with many	

Educational programmes are revised frequently, according to each child's maturation and progress. The children are given rewards for carrying out small tasks. Whenever possible, the children should choose their treats, because they may have their own ideas as to what things are 'valuable'. One child chose a wedge of abandoned crinkly paper; another chose to have time to sit near the heater!

Educational strategies are established individually on the basis of a detailed assessment of the autistic person's learning status and abilities, trying to identify potential for the acquisition of skills rather than pointing out deficits.

The assessment called PEPr, i.e. the revised Psycho Educational Profile, tries to identify areas where the person 'passes' (i.e. knows what items are used for), areas where the skill is not there yet, and areas where the skill is emerging. These domains are then put in an individual education programme (IEP). This assessment is multi-dimensional – a must, since there is great variability of skills even in the same autistic person, from one domain of competence to another. For example, a particular child may be skilled at maths yet not know how to ask to go to the toilet, so every aspect of development must be understood.

As opposed to behaviour modification, these strategies do not work on behaviour directly, but on underlying conditions that will foster learning experiences. They also make use of recent cognitive psychology research results about some differences in particular areas of brain processing in those with autism.

When behaviour problems occur, they are not treated directly or punished. Rather, the approach calls for efforts to understand the underlying reasons for each behaviour problem: anxiety, physical pain, difficulty with the task, unpredictable changes and/or boredom.

The Son-Rise programme

Son-Rise is an American home-based programme where a parent or carer interacts with the child on an intensive one-to-one basis in a setting specially designed to have few distractions. The key factor is that the carer observes the child closely and tries to build communication through copying what the child does and providing the words to describe the action. For example, the adult would say 'spin' if the child exhibited a schema of spinning a coin. The idea behind this approach is that the child, seeing the adult copy the activity, will conclude that the activity initiated by him must be very worthwhile as the adult is doing it too. This helps eye contact between child and adult. Once even brief eye contact is gained, the procedure is repeated and, over time, interactions are extended in the same way.

Applied Behaviour Analysis

Applied Behaviour Analysis (ABA) involves behaviour modification utilising part of Skinner's stimulus–response theory and an intensive one-to-one method. This combination teaches appropriate behaviours through breaking down activities into very small steps and rewarding correct responses. The method focuses on the development of personal skills. In one session, thirty or so steps may be practised. Once again the rewards should be chosen by the children, who may have very different notions as to what those rewards should be. Choices have varied from having a sticking plaster to being allowed to sit in a tent for a short time. The teacher must be able to understand the key to the children's motivation.

PECS (Picture Exchange System)

The Picture Exchange System involves the use of pictures or children's drawings of things so as to help those children who have little or no speech to communicate their wishes. For example, the children hand over a picture of a cup to show they would like a drink, and this simple exchange allows them a measure of independence. The system can be used to develop sentences.

Some academics claim that PECS is a subset of ABA – i.e. it concentrates on getting results without addressing the root of the problem. Teachers in the main (my findings) have found the system very helpful.

Both of these methods should be recorded on individual education plans. The system is home, community and school based and so success depends on cooperation among all who interact with the child. These systems are facilitators and do not claim to be cures for autism.

Different therapies suit different children and finding what is best may be frustratingly tedious and expensive. Dietary changes help some children and light and sound therapies help others. Sadly, there is no one best way that always works.

An introduction to cerebral palsy

Cerebral palsy is a complex condition that is evidenced through movement difficulties. It is a persistent but changing condition caused by damage to the brain prenatally, during birth or before 3 years of age (National Institute for Neurological Disorders and Stroke (NIND 2008)). It is not progressive in that the condition does not get worse, but maturational changes, e.g. children having to control longer limbs, and additional age-related demands on the child may make it appear so. As yet, there is no cure.

Some children are minimally affected, perhaps having a very slight impediment in walking due to a slight lack of muscle tone in one limb, but others are severely disabled by the condition. They may have painful muscle spasms and require a walking frame or wheelchair and will be totally dependent on others for their entire lives. There is not one typical child. The effects of CP are as individual as the children themselves. The syndrome is usually caused by some hazard affecting the brain so that the messages from the brain to the muscle groups do not function correctly. The brain may not have developed properly before birth or birth trauma may mean that the child has been starved of oxygen, and CP results.

The 'faulty' part is within the brain, not the muscle groups. Messages to them are often jumbled or erratic and so the children have unpredictable movements that they cannot control. As a result, the children's balance, coordination and control are all affected.

In Britain, about 1,500 babies are born with or develop CP shortly after birth. It can affect children from all ethnic groups and all social backgrounds.

Causes of cerebral palsy include:

- an infection during the first weeks of prenatal development;
- a difficult or premature birth restricting oxygen to the baby;
- failure by the baby to breathe properly;
- bleeding in the brain – most often with premature babies;
- some abnormal development within the brain for no apparent reason;
- very rarely, a genetic disorder even if both parents are clear.

However, in many cases, there is no obvious cause (Scope 2007). Specialist support in terms of physiotherapy and later speech and language therapy is vital. This should begin early so that critical learning times are not missed. The key move for the teacher is, first, to read up about the condition, then, second, to follow the same expert advice the parent follows, or if this is not known, to contact the expert working with the child. There should be no mixed messages to confuse the child. Conductive education (see 'What research is being done' at the end of this appendix) is the choice of many.

Often a group of children can join the affected child in an activity programme, e.g. in moulding clay to strengthen fingers; to lift rubber quoits with outstretched hands; to learn to sit well before beginning to draw; to stand well before walking; to do body awareness games; to blow bubbles from a soapy wand – all these exercises will benefit all children and a group activity makes the child with CP less isolated. The other children will hopefully develop empathy and respect and the children can enjoy working together, developing confidence in each other as they do. This develops a holistic approach and fosters inclusion. One wheelchair covered with golden cloth became Cinderella's coach and the other children were quite envious of the occupant!

Are there different types of cerebral palsy?

There are three main types, i.e. spastic CP, ataxic CP and athetoid CP. However, due to the complexity of the condition, it is often difficult to determine which kind a child has.

Spastic cerebral palsy, the most common kind

In this type, the muscles are contracted, i.e. stiff and tight, limiting the range of movement in the joints. This means that movements that other children do with ease are hard work. The amount and kind of activity/rest has to be advised by the physiotherapist, who will describe the condition as one of the following:

- *Hemiplegia*: In hemiplegia, half the body – either the right or the left side – is affected.
- *Diplegia*: In diplegia, both legs are affected but not the arms – or they may be very slightly affected.
- *Quadriplegia*: In quadriplegia, both arms and legs are equally affected.

The main work is to help the muscles relax so that movement can be more extensive and pain-free.

Athetoid cerebral palsy

In this type, the children's muscles change from being hypotonic (i.e. floppy, lacking tone) to being hypertonic (too tight) in an involuntary way so that the children make uncontrolled movements. Arms may flail and legs jerk and this is beyond the children's control. The children's speech can be difficult to understand because of difficulties in breath control. This can affect breathing and swallowing. Hearing problems are also common.

Ataxic cerebral palsy

In this type, achieving and maintaining balance is the main problem. Children with this type find walking difficult. They may be able to walk but have to concentrate hard to carry out the sequence and fight for balance with each step. Generally, children have uncoordinated movements. Often they have shaky hand movements and jerky speech cause by poor control of the 150 muscles in the lips, tongue and soft palate, i.e. the speech apparatus.

Is the child's intelligence affected? Will children be able to follow the curriculum?

Many children with cerebral palsy have average or even above average intelligence although their condition may hinder their ability to express or demonstrate what they know or have learned. Alternative ways of tapping into the children's knowledge base may have to be found and of course when control is affected, the children may need longer to 'show what they know'. As with any child, teachers should convey that their expectations of success are high. They should concentrate on what the children do well and so enhance their self-esteem.

What resources will the teacher need?

When children are more severely affected, walking frames and hoists will be provided. If hearing is a difficulty, using Numicon for maths and the 'look and say' method for reading will give success but of course a curriculum has to be planned to meet the specific needs of each child and has to be reviewed regularly. These methods benefit children with Down's syndrome and all other strong visual learners too.

Play activities such as working with clay to strengthen fingers and arms, baking, passing quoits to a partner all help develop muscle control and give the children confidence in their ability to do different things. It is vital that teachers notice and praise small achievements as well as major ones and remember that the effort to achieve them may have been immense.

What research is being done?

Researchers are investigating why there are mishaps in foetal brain development that result in cerebral palsy. Scientists are also looking at bleeding in the brains of newborn babies and trying to find why some should suffer epileptic seizures, and breathing and circulation problems that can cause the abnormal release of chemicals that trigger the kind of damage that causes cerebral palsy.

To make sure children are getting the right kinds of therapies, studies are also being done that evaluate both experimental treatments and treatments already in use, e.g. conductive education. This was first tried at the Peto Institute in Hungary but is now available at centres in the UK and some nursery schools where staff have been specially trained. It is essential that that physicians and parents have up-to-date, valid information to help them choose the best therapy (NIND 2008).

Conductive education is a holistic approach, originally begun at the Peto Institute in Hungary. All aspects of the child's education are built into a remedial plan and the child actively participates in a specially designed programme. There are centres in the UK but still in 2008 research is unable to claim that this method is superior to physiotherapy. However, there are many who believe that the intensity of the programme and the close relationships which form between the trainers and the children help them to progress. Google 'Conductive Education' for more details.

'With support and physiotherapy from an early age, children can learn to cope with their disability' (Scope 2007).

The Cerebral Palsy helpline offers free and confidential advice: telephone number 0800 626216 or go to www.cphelpline@scope.org.uk.

Understanding dyspraxia

Dyspraxia is one of the specific learning difficulties that impacts on every aspect of children's lives. Although people affected by dyspraxia are likely to have average or above average intelligence, there is a discrepancy in that their 'performance score' based on carrying out efficient movement patterns is surprisingly low. Just before I go on to explain that, however, I think it is worth making three important points.

The first is that there are other names for this condition and this can be confusing. Some people prefer the term DCD (developmental coordination disorder); others, mainly in Scandinavia, call it DAMP (disorder of attention, movement and perception), and this certainly covers the learning process, but in education in the UK we use the term dyspraxia because it sits alongside dyslexia and dyscalculia, commonly used and well understood terms in schools, and indeed children with these conditions very often have movement difficulties too. Children with dyspraxia used to be called 'the clumsy ones' but that sounded as though if they just tried harder they could overcome their difficulties, and this is untrue. They need understanding and positive support from everyone – including physiotherapists and speech therapists if speech is unclear. Poor muscle tone in the mouth can cause difficulties with articulation. These children are likely to be trying just as hard as they can.

The second point is that dyspraxic difficulties are on a continuum, with some children much less affected than others. Some children appear 'just a little bit clumsy', perhaps knocking things over or tripping over thin air, while for others, to quote Alex, 'It's like trying to walk through thick mud or trying to write with boxing gloves on.' This variation means that there is not one typical child with dyspraxia. Diagnosis is tricky because tests of motor ability do not provide cut-off points between those who have and those who do not have the condition. This means that although parents and teachers may have their suspicions, experts in the field have to be called in to make any formal diagnosis. Usually the decision depends on whether the children's lives are significantly affected by the condition.

The third point concerns duration. Does dyspraxia go away as the children grow? Sadly, the answer is 'No' but with regular support and practice all the children can be helped. It is vitally important that planned, positive input comes as early as possible because that is when remediation is most effective.

What is dyspraxia?

The name gives us a clue, for 'dys' means faulty and 'praxis' is the ability to plan and use effective movement or the ability to use the body as a skilled tool. So there are two aspects to be considered:

1 The thinking, planning, organising and sequencing or the intellectual side of moving, which also involves remembering how to do things.
2 Actually being able to carry out the movement itself. This is the physical or the 'doing' side and efficiency depends on the child having enough strength, balance, coordination and control.

There is a subtle way in which poor memory may influence effective movement and this is called habituation. If a child without dyspraxia attempts to run and jump over a puddle and lands right in it, then next time he will adjust his speed so that he travels further or he'll take off nearer the edge; in other words, he will use feedback from the first try to improve the next, and when he gets it right, then this pattern is set into his memory. On a subsequent try, this is recalled and the correct pattern is carried out. But children with dyspraxia don't seem to be able to do this; they have to carry out each action as a first-time try. Remember what learning to drive was like? And yet once you could do it, the skill was held in your procedural memory and it became automatic. Imagine if this didn't happen. Imagine how tired and cross you might be? When this goes on all day, life becomes very difficult. This is dyspraxia and it is not difficult to imagine how it impacts on children's confidence, especially in new situations when directions and distances are confusing, and changing routines hold not interest and challenge, but confusion and fear.

These difficulties are exacerbated at transition times between schools, especially when children leave the relatively sheltered junior school to go to secondary. There the distances and directions to move between classes can be very confusing. Classes are made up of different children who do not appreciate the difficulties children with dyspraxia have. Unfortunately, this coincides with adolescence and the children also having to cope with the hormonal onslaught that brings.

The early signs

So why should some children not be able to do the things we take for granted and how early is it possible to spot these difficulties?

One of the earliest signs is that the baby is hypotonic, i.e. showing poor muscle tone. Mums say, 'I knew from the start there was something wrong, he was so floppy', and this lack of strength becomes even more evident when the baby is late in achieving his motor milestones. Children with dyspraxia will walk and run and jump but later than normal and at the lower end of competence. It is likely that crawling using the cross-lateral pattern will be missed and parents and practitioners must check this and encourage children to adopt it, because crawling sets up a template in the brain that eases later learning.

Children with dyspraxia have difficulties with balance, coordination and control. These are the key difficulties that should be supported first.

The 'poor balance' that is an important part of dyspraxia may even have affected the baby before and during birth. In the womb the senses are beginning to work and the vestibular sense (the first sense to be myelinated and the leader of the sensory orchestra) gets the baby in the head-down position, ready to be born. If the vestibular sense is not working properly and as a result the baby is in the breech or transverse position, then there may have to be a Caesarean section birth. If the child is later found to have dyspraxia, the mum may blame the birth process, but actually it was likely to be the case that the baby's sense of balance was not functioning well. So it is vital to check this and prepare all sorts of simple activities to encourage it.

A key paediatrician has claimed, 'When we understand balance, we'll understand the aetiology of everything.' Balance is fundamental in everything we do.

Many children with dyspraxia will have great difficulty in doing many of the activities of daily living, e.g. using a knife and fork, doing up buttons or writing neatly, because they have a retained primitive reflex called the ATNR (the asymmetric tonic neck reflex). Children who have this will not have crawled using the cross-lateral pattern, i.e. one hand moving forward, then the opposite knee. They may have bum-shuffled or gone from sitting to walking. Parents may think they have done well to miss a step but many children that didn't crawl, couldn't crawl. So an early check can be made by encouraging children to crawl. It's interesting to note that many children with handwriting difficulties didn't or couldn't crawl.

A further difficulty in dyspraxia is poor body and spatial awareness. If children don't feel where their body parts are without looking, it is difficult to control them. Their proprioceptors (nerve endings in the muscle groups) may not be relaying the correct level of impulse to the brain or the brain may not be sending accurate messages to the limbs. One highly intelligent 10-year-old, explaining his very poor writing, said, 'I can see in my head what I want my hands to do but when it comes down to my hands it goes all wrong somehow.' How frustrating was that? Children with dyspraxia need support in helping them develop their balance, their coordination and their control.

So why is movement so important? Does it really matter if children can't ride a bike or tie their laces at the same time as their friends? Of course it does. Their confidence and self-esteem take a huge knock when they are last to get dressed, when they hate PE and football, and when everyone gets cross and tells them to hurry up, it's no wonder that they cry. Often in school they will try to disguise their problems by copying other children or pretending they don't care but when they get home they explode and the parents take the brunt of their frustration.

Jingles that prompt movement and knowing body parts, e.g. Tap Time, are to be found in *Jingle Time* by Christine Macintyre (2003). A favourite jingle, 'Tap Time', is given in Appendix 7.

Although it's easiest to observe dyspraxia in the large movements, we have to remember that speech may be affected too. It may be in articulating words or coordinating the rhythm of sounds. This requires coordination of 150 muscles in the lips, soft palate and the tongue, so floppiness there means that speaking clearly or eating in a socially approved, lips closed manner is difficult. Some children with dyspraxia have a co-occurring Tourette's syndrome – they have explosions of sound that they can't control.

Gross motor performance may be better than the execution of fine motor skills if the musculature in the top part of the body is more severely affected. Writing or drawing within lines or placing figures in boxes in a maths jotter can be very difficult for children with dyspraxia, so texts and papers need to accommodate this.

And there are other linked difficulties. Poor muscle tone leads to slouching, which can affect breathing and make other 'workings' sluggish, so digestive difficulties and constipation may occur. And if the muscles behind the eyes don't work together, focussing on a task can become very tiring, even painful. This may be Mears-Irlen syndrome, now called visual stress, which can be overcome by using coloured overlays or spectacles. These should be chosen by an optician specialising in colour therapy. Then, if the sphincter that controls flow from the bladder is weak, poor toilet control can have devastating effects.

Some children exhibit a very strange running pattern. If the muscles around the hips are not strong enough for the child to control a forward transference of weight pattern, this means the child can't run fast enough to play and he can't kick a ball with any control. As movement competence is public, open to peer assessment, can you see how this affects his confidence?

Observation can be tricky because some children are adept at disguising their difficulties. They use one sense to compensate for the difficulties using another. But when movements become more challenging and/or support is reduced, then the difficulties can affect all the activities of daily living.

The study of perception or how the senses take in information from the environment is a complex study on its own, but it is important to consider how each of the senses work singly and together in a study of dyspraxia. Very briefly, the vestibular sense or sense of balance is part of everything we do and if children have a poor sense of balance, then everything is affected. The visual sense is of course for seeing but also for discriminating details. It is also important for tracking the flight of a ball or the words on a page. Similarly, the auditory sense, primarily for hearing, needs to be sharp enough to discriminate the sounds of language and also to have the facility to cut out distracters in the environment when this is appropriate. The tactile sense or feeling/touching sense is particularly important in dyspraxia, for some children are hypo-sensitive – they can't bear to be touched; they even feel pain when they have their hair or nails cut, and seams in socks or clothes can be intolerable. So checking how the children experience their sensory input is an important part of diagnosis.

Incidence: the numbers affected by dyspraxia

The Dyspraxia Foundation has given the statistic that 6–10 per cent of all children have some degree of dyspraxia, so there will be affected children in every class. Boys outnumber girls in the ratio of 4:1, but when girls are dyspraxic, they are often more severely affected. See also Macintyre (2003, 2009).

All the movement activities referred to throughout the text will support children with dyspraxic difficulties. These should be done as often as possible when the children are fresh, and must be fun, not relegated to tiresome exercises!

Dyslexia

There are many definitions of dyslexia in current use and this can cause confusion for parents, teachers and the children themselves. The British Dyslexia Association (BDA), cited in Everatt and Reid (2009), suggest:

> Dyslexia is a combination of abilities and difficulties that affect the learning process in one or more of reading, spelling and writing. Accompanying weaknesses may be identified in areas of speed of processing, short-term memory, sequencing, auditory and/or visual perception, spoken language and motor skills. It is particularly related to mastering and using written language which may include alphabetic, numeric and musical notation.

This comprehensive definition might be considered somewhat daunting, but parents and teachers have to remember that not all children will have all these difficulties. Sometimes giving more time can be a useful first step. Then the personal difficulties can be more readily identified.

The quotation from the BDA shows that dyslexia, like dyspraxia, is a specific learning difficulty, i.e. the child's difficulties are not generalised but are specific to one area that nonetheless can impinge on other areas of learning. Early identification of this learning difference is imperative, because early intervention can be effective and point the way to appropriate curricular modifications later on. But teachers have to remember that it is never too late to support children with these difficulties, and indeed adults, because their learning differences might not have been recognised when they were at school. Importantly, dyslexia should not be regarded as something that will limit learning potential. In fact, children and adults with dyslexia can have an advantage in visual tasks and do very well in creative and problem-solving activities. Winston (2004) explains that dyslexia is not related to intelligence and endorses the claim that 'Many people with dyslexia have made sterling contributions to the fields of architecture, medicine, art and literature.' He claims that the relation between sight and perception is the most variable. He shows that one pathway in the visual mechanism is different and this leads to a slower processing mechanism. Many children find words moving on the page, thus confusing their reading. Research by Livingstone *et al.* (1991) at the Harvard Medical School showed that neurones in the fast layers of the thalamus, dealing with movement and location, were more disorganised in dyslexics.

Many students with dyslexia (now termed a learning difference rather than a disability) experience difficulties in phonological processing, but these vary from one to the other. This means that a range of ways in teaching children with dyslexia need to be considered.

Early signs

In pre-school children

Dyslexia is a specific learning difficulty focussing on literacy skills. The children affected by dyslexia have many attributes – they are often creative and imaginative and just as (orally) bright as their peers – yet there is 'something' that prevents these able children making progress. When children show a cluster of the following difficulties, then action must be taken, for in these early years, much can be done.

Some of the difficulties can be seen in all children, but in dyslexic children they stand out more and may be more resistant to intervention than in other children. It is important not to jump to conclusions too early, for progress in learning can be erratic at this early stage. What then are the difficulties?

Difficulty in:

- learning nursery rhymes;
- paying attention when listening to a story;
- keeping still – always restless;
- being slow to speak;
- keeping simple rhythms;
- forgetting names of objects or people;
- moving around without tripping or bumping;
- cutting out – difficulty in handling scissors or threading accurately;
- remembering instructions, but can act upon one at a time;
- getting dressed – especially fastening buttons;
- catching and kicking a ball;
- hopping and/or skipping.

When children are identified as dyslexic, they require support in

- speech and language;
- movement skills;
- memory skills;
- auditory and possibly visual perception.

Later difficulties

Primary school age

In primary age children, the literacy side of the curriculum is affected, with possibly some numeric difficulty. Sports and movement activities may not be enjoyed but, that said, some children are very able sportspeople.

Some general observations:

- slow speed of processing information;
- slow spoken and/or written language;
- has difficulty following more than one instruction;
- forgets names/words.

Writing

Dyslexic children often have problems with writing:

- The child will be likely to have a surprisingly low standard of written work – messy work with many scorings out.
- The child is confused (for a long time) by letters that look similar, e.g. m/w, b/d, n/u, p/g.
- Reversing letters is common – lasting much longer than the phase many children pass through.
- The child spells the same word differently in the same piece of writing.
- The child may use unusual sequences of words.
- The child has poor handwriting; the fingers may be too relaxed or too rigid, preventing flow.
- The child's writing doesn't stay close to the margin – poor presentation skills.

Reading

Generally poor progress, especially using look and say methods. The child will have problems with reading. They experience difficulties in:

- hearing the difference in sounds;
- blending letters together;
- pronouncing certain words;
- appreciating syllable division;
- being expressive when reading;
- picking out the key issues in a story;
- reading every word – they miss some or add others;
- recognising familiar words;
- reading aloud, especially in a group.

Number

When counting, the child has difficulties in:

- keeping 'hundreds, tens and units' separate;
- remembering the order of events, e.g. days of the week, months of the year;
- learning to tell the time;
- understanding abstract concepts, e.g. yesterday, tomorrow.

Time/personal organisation

Difficulties in:

- learning to tell the time and appreciating its use;
- remembering the day of the week and what happens then;
- getting ready in time with books organised;
- understanding the passage of time, e.g. 'finish in five minutes . . .'.

Movement skills

Difficulties in

- balance, coordination and control;
- pencil control;
- sitting steadily at the desk (check the height of the desk and whether the child's feet are steady on the floor);
- understanding directional words, e.g. forwards, backwards, opposite, etc.;
- hand/foot dominance – the child may be unsure which hand/foot to use.

Behaviour

Difficulties in:

- keeping on task – uses avoidance strategies (toilet, sharpening pencil, etc.);
- staying fresh – children get very tired with constant concentration;
- not assuming roles such as the class clown (cries for recognition).

Of course, not all children have all the difficulties mentioned above – each child will have a specific profile that needs careful monitoring and adjustment as progress is shown.

When a child does not make the progress expected in the light of his oral competence, teachers need to compile an individual educational profile (IEP). This should highlight any areas of competence as well as patterns of errors, so that the child's self-esteem can be enhanced. Teachers might consider whether the child has difficulty in recognising the link between letters and sounds or blending difficulties, i.e. separating words into sounds and blending the sounds to form words. Checks should be made that the child can decode single words without contextual cues such as pictures, for often children can remember the picture and guess the word. Perhaps the child reads slowly and laboriously without expression because the effort to read takes away the meaning of what is expressed? Then decoding difficulties can be explored. Another assessment procedure should ask if, say, oral spelling can be substituted for written work. This would show the child's level of understanding not contaminated by difficulty in writing or blending. Drama activities are other ways of assessing understanding. Many children can show understanding through movement, i.e. using their kinaesthetic sense, which is not impaired by dyslexia. But above all, talk is a prime mechanism for giving children success. This is an active form of learning where children with dyslexia can show what they have learned. And so there are ways to assess the children beyond reading and writing and spelling. Using these measures will enhance the children's confidence and let them shine!

The movement component of dyslexia is often not given enough priority in my view because a good sense of balance is essential, and a link to the way letters are written is being researched. Also, the coordination to write can be helped by paying attention to the height of the desk and chair and to the suitability of the writing implement. So again the first set of 'things to be considered' are simple ones. Then, once these have been dealt with, there are many tests to provide a detailed diagnosis.

Some examples of standardised tests are:

* the Wechsler Intelligence Scale (WISC IV);
* the Wechsler Individual Achievement Test;
* Edinburgh Reading tests/Moray House test, University of Edinburgh;
* the Bangor Dyslexia Screening test;
* the Cognitive Profiling System (CoPs);
* the Dyslexia Early Screening test;
* the Special Needs Assessment Profile.

The profile (SNAP) is a computer-aided diagnostic assessment and profiling package (by Charles Weedon and Gavin Reid 2003, 2005, 2009). This can suggest a diagnosis that points the way to an individual teaching programme for individual children. The website is www.SNAPassessment.com.

Tap Time and Sensations

Tap Time

Tap on your head and
Clap, clap, clap
Tap on your knees and
Flap, flap, flap.
Look all around you
Who do you see?
Wave to them, run and
Join two hands
And jump, 2, 3!

(Children now in twos facing one another)

Tap on their shoulders
Clap, clap, clap
Tap on their elbows
Flap, flap, flap.
Look all around you
Who do you see?
Join up in a threesome
And jump 2, 3.

Stretch out and make your circle
Wide, wide, wide.
Make it very small again
Who is by your side?
Join up with another three
How many now?
Make your circle spin around
Then take a bow!

Sensations

Smoothly, smoothly stroke a tiny kitten.
Softly, softly, just lightly touch its fur,
Gently, gently, you don't want to be bitten.
Listen to it purr.
Jaggy jaggy, running on the sand now.
Prickly, prickly, these little stones do cling,
Razor shells with lots of raggy edges,
No wonder that they sting!
Stiffly, stiffly, march around the room now.
Make your arms and legs stay straight,
Salute your friend as you march past now.
'Halt' means stop and wait!
Softly, softly, it's time to go to bed now,
Cuddle down, you'll soon be nice and warm.
Dream a dream and have a little sleep now,
Safe from any harm.

Jingle Time (Macintyre 2003)

Bibliography

Argyle, M. (1962) *Bodily Communication*, London: Methuen.

Arron, J. (2006) 'NFAT dysregulation by increased dosage of DSCRI1 and DYRKIA on chromosome 21', *Nature*, 441: 595–9.

Baron-Cohen, R. (1991) 'The development of a theory of mind in autism: deviance and delay?' *Psychiatric Clinics of North America*, 14: 33–51.

Beetlestone, F. (1998) *Creative Children, Imaginative Teaching*, Buckingham: Open University Press.

Buzan, T. (2006) *Mind Mapping*, London: Buzanworld Publishing.

Carter, R. (2004) *Mapping the Mind*, London: Phoenix Books.

Cohen, D. (1979) *The Development of Play*, New York: HarperCollins.

Corlett, L. (2006) *Attention Deficit Hyperactivity Disorder: A Guide to Intervention and Management of Pupils with ADHD*, Edinburgh: City of Edinburgh Psychological Service, Merchiston Park.

Cumine, V., Leach, J. and Stevenson, G. (2007) *Autism in the Early Years*, Oxon: Routledge.

Donaldson, M. (1978) *Children's Minds*, London: Fontana.

Everatt, J. and Reid, G. (2009) 'An overview of recent research', in G. Reid (ed.) *The Routledge Companion to Dyslexia*, London: Routledge.

Gardner, H. (1983) *Frames of Mind: The Theory of Multiple Intelligences*, Cambridge, MA: Harvard University Press.

Gardner, H. (2007) *Five Minds for the Future*, Cambridge, MA: Harvard University Press.

Goddard Blythe, S. (2005) *The Well Balanced Child*, Stroud: Hawthorn Press.

Gray, C. (1996) 'Social stories and comic strip conversations with students with Asperger's syndrome and high functioning autism', in E. Schopler, G.B. Mesibov and L. Kunce (eds) *Asperger's Syndrome and High Functioning Autism*, New York: Plenum Press.

Gurney, P. (1987) 'Self-esteem enhancement in children: a review of research findings', *Educational Research*, 29(2): 130–6.

Huttenlocher, J. (1998) Language input and language growth', *Preventive Medicine*, 27: 195–9.

Isaacs, S. (1933) *Social Development in Young Children*, London: Routledge.

Isaacson, R. (2009) *The Horse Boy: A Father's Miraculous Journey to Heal his Son*, London: Viking.

Jackson, L. (2002) *Freaks, Geeks and Asperger's Syndrome: A User's Guide to Adolescence*. London: Jessica Kingsley Publishers.

Jordan, R. and Powell, S. (1995) *Understanding and Teaching Children with Autism*, London: Wiley.

Kanner, L. (1943) 'Autistic disturbances of affective contact', *Nervous Child*, 2: 217–50.

Keen, D. (2001) 'Specific developmental disorders', paper presented at the conference on the Needs of Children with Coordination Disorders, Bishop Auckland, February.

Keen, D. and Ward, S. (2004) *Autistic Spectrum Disorders: A Child Population Profile*, London: Sage.

Kirby, A. and Drew, S. (2003) *Guide to Dyspraxia and Developmental Coordination Disorders*, London: David Fulton Publishers.

Kuhl, P.K. (2000) 'A new view of language acquisition', *Proceedings of the National Academy of Science of the United States of America*, 97: 11850–7.

Livingstone, M.S., Rosen, G.D., Drislane, F.W. and Galaburda, A.M. (1991) 'Physiological and anatomical evidence for a magnocellular defect in developmental dyslexia', *Proceedings of the National Academy of Sciences of the United States of America*, 88: 7943–7.

Macintyre, C. (2003) *Jingle Time*, Abingdon: David Fulton Publishers.

Macintyre, C. (2008) *Dyspraxia in the Early Years*, 2nd edn, Oxon: Routledge.

Macintyre, C. (2009) *Dyspraxia 5–14*, 2nd edn, Oxon: Routledge.

Macintyre, C. and Deponio, P. (2003) *Assessing and Supporting Children with Specific Learning Difficulties: Looking beyond the Label to Assess the Whole Child*, London: Routledge.

Macintyre, C. and McVitty, K. (2003) *Planning the Pre-5 Setting*, Abingdon: David Fulton Publishers.

Moore, C. (2004) *George and Sam*, London: Viking.

Neihart, M. (2003) 'Gifted children with Attention Deficit Hyperactivity Disorder', ERIC EC Digest 649, *Journal of the Support for Learning Association* (ILSA) Dublin.

Paley, V.G. (2005) *A Child's Work: The Importance of Fantasy Play*, Chicago: University of Chicago Press.

Palmer, S. (2006) *Toxic Childhood*, London: Orion.

Palmer, S. and Bailey, R. (2004) *Foundations of Literacy*, Stafford: Network Educational Press.

Peer, L. (2002) 'Otitis media: a new hypothesis in dyslexia?' Paper presented at the BDA International Conference, University of Warwick.

Pope, M. (1988) *Dyspraxia: A Head Teacher's Perspective*, Hitchin: The Dyspraxia Trust.

Reid, G. (2005) 'Specific learning difficulties: the spectrum', in N. Jones (ed.) *Developing School Provision for Children with Dyspraxia*, London: Paul Chapman.

Reilly, M. (1974) *Play as Exploratory Learning*, Beverly Hills, CA: Sage.

Rios, M.V. (2000) 'Living with contradictions', in *Uniquely Gifted: Identifying and Meeting the Needs of the Twice-Exceptional Student*, Gilsum, NH: Avocus Publishing.

Rush, E. (1997) 'Managing the dyspraxic child through sensory integration therapy', conference paper presented at Appleford School, Shrewton.

Scope (2007) *What is Cerebral Palsy?* London: Scope.

Stern, S. (2007) 'Mental building blocks for the next century', *Financial Times*, 28 March, available at: http://www.ft.com/home/uk.

Trevarthen, C. (1977) *Play for Tomorrow*, video production, Edinburgh University.

Vygotsky, L. (1978) *Mind and Society*, Cambridge, MA: Harvard University Press.

Weedon, C. and Reid, G. (2003) *Special Needs Assessment Portfolio*, London: Hodder and Stoughton, version 2, 2005; version 3, 2009.

Wikipedia (2008) Down syndrome, available at: http://en.wikipedia.org/wiki/Down_syndrome.

Winkley, D (2004) ' "Grey matters": current neurological research and its implications for educators', available at: http://www.keele.ac.uk/depts/ed/kisnet/interviews/winkley/htm.

Winslow, L. (2007) 'Dyslexia and over-achievers in society', 2 February. Available at: *Ezine Articles.com*. http://ezinearticles.com/?Dyslexia-and-Over-Achievers-in-Society&id= 439726 (accessed 17 Aug. 2009).

Winston, R. (2004) *The Human Mind*, New York: Bantam Books.

Wishart, J. (2006) Extract from paper given at Edinburgh University entitled 'Understanding Down's Syndrome'.

Index

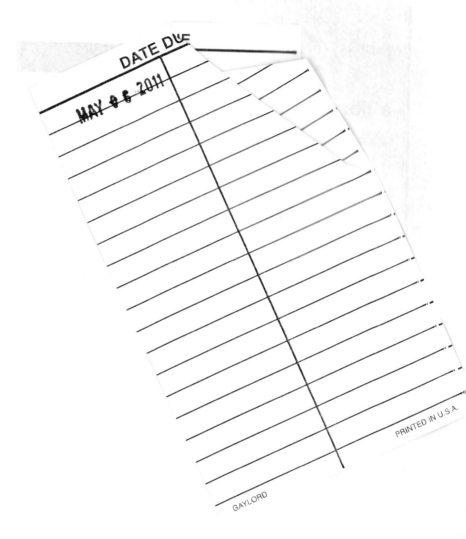

DATE DUE

MAY 0 6 2011

PRINTED IN U.S.A.

GAYLORD